Praise for *Social PR Secrets*

Leading the way from traditional to 'Social PR,' Lisa's expertise and proven methods empower PR and marketing professionals to successfully leverage today's social, digital landscape to promote the brand. A must-have reference!

Rebecca Murtagh, CEO, speaker, and author of *Million Dollar Websites: Build a Better Website Using Best Practices of the Web Elite* @virtualmarketer

Effective public relations execution continues to evolve, especially in the high-tech software industry. Social PR Secrets, is packed full of actionable, real world tactics that we put to use in our company with immediate results. My team found the numerous nuggets of information in the book to be easy to read and act upon. It's a must read for your PR or marketing team.

Ron Antevy, President and CEO e-Builder, Inc. an SaaS company @ebuilder

Extremely informative and designed for those marketing professionals who, like me, have a short attention span. Social PR Secrets, is a must read! The online public relations industry continues to evolve as fast—if not faster—then the digital space itself. Whether you are representing yourself or your clients online, Lisa is the perfect guide when it comes to informative tips and strategies on delivering company news outside the traditional journalism ecosystem across social media, mobile devices, and visual press releases—all of which must be optimized for search engines.

Matt McGowan, Managing Director, Incisive Media @matt_mcgowan

SOCIAL PR SECRETS

How to Optimize, Socialize, and Publicize
Your Brand's News

LISA BUYER

Hashtag: #SocialPRSecrets

Social PR Secrets doesn't stop here. Join the conversation by
following the #Hashtag #SocialPRSecrets or check out these
websites for updates of Lisa Buyer's PR Secrets' publications
and events: socialprsecrets.com or lisabuyer.com

Illustrations by Lauren Litwinka
facebook.com/deepcereal
@beebow

Dedication

There have been many lives and many masters in my life. This book is dedicated to my dad, he always wanted to write a book about his memoirs, and to Tracy, she never dreamed her life would be cut short and there would be a book about her death.

To my mom, she proofed this book and my life.

Contents

Foreword by Sarah Evans, Digital Correspondent and author of *[Re]frame: Little Inspirations for a Larger Purpose* xi

Introduction 1

Chapter 1
Social PR Evolution 3

Chapter 2
Social PR Revolution 6

Chapter 3
Today's Media Relations... 12

Chapter 4
The New Press Release 17

Chapter 5
Content Strategy 23

Chapter 6
Editorial Calendar 28

Chapter 7
Online Newsrooms.. 35

Chapter 8
The Art and Science of Social Publishing 40

Chapter 9
Managing A Community... 44

Chapter 10
Jump Into Any News Story... 49

Chapter 11
Distribution and Amplification 54

Chapter 12
Mobile and Social PR Hook Up 61

Chapter 13
The Rise of Visual Reporting 65

Chapter 14
Scoring Influence 70

Chapter 15
Measurement, Analytics, and Google 76

Chapter 16
Avoiding a PR Disaster 82

Chapter 17
Strategy for Tragedy 86

Chapter 18
Social PR Wisdom 91

About the Author 96

#SocialPRSecrets Twitter List 98

Foreword

BY SARAH EVANS, DIGITAL CORRESPONDENT AND AUTHOR

Lisa Buyer painstakingly practices what she preaches. She's a doer, an experimenter, and is constantly learning so she can remain the PR trendmaster that she is. Her dedication to online servant leadership, freely offering so much of her knowledge, is what you get in real life, too. She's a true example of the modern day PR professional—a digital nomad with the ability to think like a producer and editor and be the consummate brand advocate.

Whether it's media relations, social strategy, or internal communications, companies are looking for more efficient and effective ways to use emerging and established technologies.

If you work in a slow moving, behemoth of a company, small victories—like establishing a Facebook page—are the result of months, if not years, of campaigning. For those who are in smaller or more agile companies, you may be the frontrunners, jumping on new technologies as they become available. Either way, you're likely tasked with staying in-the-know and monitoring all things social.

Consider Social PR Secrets the communication professional's modern-day beginner's handbook. It may appear to have a light-hearted or whimsical approach, but therein lies its brilliance. The non-threatening format allows anyone to feel comfortable reading while they are exposed to tactical and practical public relations tips.

Trying to learn all the nuances and theories of search and optimization, social and publicity takes years of work, and that doesn't include all of the trial and error during stages of tactical application. And because things change quickly, what you learn could change in an instant. It requires daily diligence to stay on top of your craft.

Lisa thoughtfully lays out some of the more common roles the PR person of today plays, from the editorial to managing online communities to reporting results. At the very least, the book provides you with a realistic view of the communications landscape and at the most, shares some of the most valuable information you can use. Right. Now.

I challenge you to make Social PR Secrets a personalized guide for how you work. Treat it as your baseline, ready to help you grow faster than you could without it. Make notes in the margins, challenge what you read, or better yet, share your experiences with others (#SocialPRSecrets).

It's an exciting time to work in the communications industry. We are in a time of constant change, but some things will always remain the same. We exist to connect a brand with their stakeholders, keep consumers coming back, and to share stories.

@prsarahevans

Acknowledgments

Special thanks to the publishing pros who crossed my path and played a role in getting this book from point A to B to P for Publish: Willem Knibbe, Acquisitions Editor at Sybex, an imprint of Wiley publishing; Casey Bankord, Slimbooks co-founder; and the editorial services of Elliot Haught and Chris O'Byrne, president of JETLAUNCH.

I had a ton of collective advice from authors who shared their book-writing tips and war stories with me and helped encourage and guide me along the way. Huggable thanks to Marty Weintraub, Greg Jarboe, Mel Carson, Ric Dragon, Krista Neher, Rebecca Murtagh, and those authors that I follow for inspiration and style. Likeable thanks to Gretchen Rubin, Tony Robbins, Tony Hsieh, and Elizabeth Gilbert.

The business and life mentors that have helped shape me over the years: Dan Chiodo, Uncle Carl, and Paige Rose.

Even though he says, "Lisa, you have no idea how annoying this is," when I was proofing the final formatting of this book on the way to the UM versus UF game, thanks to the love of my life, Don, for always believing in me and supporting me even when I push the envelope of being on my computer and working at crazy times.

Charley Gilkey, my business coach, helped me carve out the time and clear the clutter to get this book from none to done. Navah Berg, Leah Fein, Victoria Edwards, Carah von Funk, and Miranda Miller—thanks for being part of the behind the scenes proofing, cheering, and positive support.

Christi, Tommy, and Tammy, my BFFs.

To the ones who evolved with me from traditional PR past to the social PR present! Cindy Metzler and Ryan Roth—you girls rock!

Introduction

Today, news happens in a tweet—instant, clear, and to the point. The entire public relations (PR) industry is evolving thanks to the search and social media revolution. PR professionals now find themselves in a new era.

Companies have an incredible opportunity to exhibit more control over the delivery of their own news content. They can be the news, share the news, and make themselves part of any mainstream or breaking story. Brands are now their own media publishers, finding that earning search results on the first page of Google, or scoring a social endorsement whether a +1, like, share, ♥, or comment, can be as influential as a traditional, front-page newspaper story.

PR professionals are the new editors, mobile photographers, brand journalists and publishers. *Social PR Secrets* uncovers how PR and online marketing professionals can use the latest social PR news-making strategies to gain more organic visibility, influence media, and directly reach their target markets. Every chapter in *Social PR Secrets* is packed with insider tips, tactics, and systems presented in tweet-sized bites for simplicity, easy reading, and sharing.

Welcome to the future of PR and marketing. It's now.

Chapter 1
Social PR Evolution

Have You Tried Google?

I'll never forget the day in 2000 that one of my employees popped into my office with a question, "Have you tried Google?" Those days, my PR agency was already immersed in all things digital, working in the go-go dot-com days. Therefore, we were curious to learn.

My traditional PR background meant a heavy focus on generating print and broadcast media coverage for emerging technology clients. Before the digital days, everything revolved around print press releases, media tours, and trade shows. The journalist was the gatekeeper and the key—and still is, in many ways—to generating publicity through their coverage of a story. Working with dot-com technology start-ups in the boom, the generation of editorial coverage meant the difference between a company impressing the investment community enough to get funded or going under in obscurity.

PR campaigns for dot-com start-ups moved at a fast and furious clip; what had once taken months to plan and execute was now reduced to weeks or even days. News began to surface faster, thanks to search engines like Yahoo! and Google. We discovered tricks in press release distribution that helped us not only reach journalists in a more direct way, but also deliver news directly to certain online segments and groups. The early days of optimization meant adding a stock symbol to an online press release to automatically land it in the email inbox of investors tracking that company. Similarly, using links in a digital press release would assist in search visibility and the delivery of traffic to that website. In the ticker symbol example, you might see how this compares to the way hashtags are used today in social media news messaging and how we can target the "likes" and "interests" of users in Facebook, for example. The most basic digital targeting and efficiencies helped us understand the opportunity in those early days.

As search engines evolved (and Google became a household name), marketers raced to figure out ways to climb to the top of search results. Meanwhile, the dot-com boom bombed and September 11, 2001 tragedies happened, sending the entire business community into a state of shock. PR professionals began to be perceived as a luxury to businesses who were asking, "What is the ROI?" "How could you prove it?" "What were organizations actually getting from all this editorial coverage?" "Was it all just fluff?"

In reality, traditional PR is hard to measure and justify. Thanks to the Internet, digital public relations became the clear winner in terms of leveling the playing fields and creating opportunities for small and large brands. The key to successful PR now lies in understanding how to balance the optimization of news content for search engines, social media, and human readers. Google News began serving up company press releases some time ago, and systems such as Google Alerts allow us to monitor industry news, competitor mentions, and our own brand mentions.

Marketers flocked to this new opportunity. The PR industry had a rebirth to garner incredible results for clients through a working knowledge of the basic practices of search engine marketing and optimization. Editorial coverage from various online news sources ranked in Google meant public relations had a new set of key performance indicators (KPIs): online visibility, ranking in search engine results, and the influence and referral of quality visitors to a website.

Have You Heard of Facebook?

Sarah Van Elzen asked me, "Have you heard of Facebook?" in January of 2007 after her graduation from the University of Minnesota. She was in her first week as an interactive PR coordinator. Active on Facebook as a student, Sarah gave me the social heads up—that is, to "ditch MySpace and check out Facebook."

After a little experimenting, I discovered Facebook was not just a social network for college kids. It had the potential to become a massive PR media outlet, giving brands a way to socialize the news message, share news, and influence publicity online coverage—and it certainly has. By late 2007, Facebook had more than 100,000 business pages. It soon became a key component in the social PR process to set up a new client with a Facebook Business Page, YouTube channel, and relative social media profiles. In addition to gaining publicity within the social networks, applying search engine optimization (SEO) best practices to social media profiles carried the added bonus of helping companies secure positive branded search results.

Are You on Twitter?

This was the big question at Pubcon 2007, where I was really geeking my way out of the traditional public relations world and entering a new solar system with planets such as Google, Facebook, and Twitter. I joined Twitter right before the conference and began following news about the speakers and sessions. The keyword here is "news," as Twitter had quickly become yet another opportunity for PR pros to report and share news digitally and in real-time. Engagement and interaction were huge factors, even in those early days. Tweeting became an essential part of the social PR arsenal.

Chapter 2
Social PR Revolution

What does Google have to do with PR?

I attended my first Search Engine Strategies (SES) conference in December 2006. I remember calling a friend right after Danny Sullivan's "Intro to Search Marketing" session and saying that I felt like I had just received my MBA. The opportunity for PR to not only capitalize on search, but to actually influence it, opened my eyes to a new world of possibilities.

Everything in search at that time was about content, and still is. When you think about it, everything in public relations is about content—via a press release, media story, blog post, image, or executive bio. The success of any given campaign largely depends on the efficacy of content in attracting attention and influencing a particular outcome. I became addicted to learning this new way of marketing and understanding how I could apply it to my public relations practice, ideally helping clients translate this into their own business success.

A complete newbie to the online marketing scene, it was in 2007 that I launched myself into finding ways to educate myself in the best practices on Internet marketing. It was horrifying to find out that the new website I had just launched was not SEO-friendly, although beautifully built in Flash. Ugh! It was hard for me to give my business card out until I had changed my website to HTML and started a blog. Not only did I believe this would be the new way of doing PR, but I also wanted to differentiate my agency in our PR service offerings. I immediately connected with online PR pros Lee Odden and Greg Jarboe, both SES speakers, and still remember attending Dana Todd's "PPC 101" (pay-per-click) session. I felt inspired at how she took the complicated subject of PPC, and made it easy to understand the process of setting up Google Ads using keywords. This new world actually helped me learn new ways to make headlines stand out in search and to inspire a user to click through to a full story. I decided to get my Google AdWords certification for the value it would have to my PR career, but also to fine-tune my search engine knowledge.

Blogging for PR

Discovering how easy it was to start a blog using platforms like Blogger or WordPress, coupled with my new SEO knowledge, meant blogs became a staple in my public relations weapon arsenal. In 2007, a PR and marketing audit for an IT client led to a recommendation that they should start a blog as a means to educate the industry as a thought leader. The CEO thought it was brilliant, yet senior management could not get their heads around why they would give out free information to the public. Thankfully, that was then and attitudes have since changed substantially. More than 60% of companies now have corporate blogs, and most understand the value of thought leadership, authenticity, transparency, and visibility.

Source:

http://blogging.org/blog/blogging-stats-2012-infographic/

"Social Media is All Fun and Games, But We Need to do Real PR"

That email came from a client back in 2008 as we were setting up YouTube channels, Facebook Pages, and social news networks as part of its PR strategy. If that client had only seen the opportunity, the gains as an early social media adapter would have been incredible! Simply having a Facebook Page was once good PR. Getting quality fans and followers was much easier and less expensive because there was little competition. Today, a successful social presence as part of an overarching PR strategy is deeper and more comprehensive. The opportunities are greater than ever, but so is the competition.

Telling an Influential Blogger to F*** Off

Six months into joining the conversation on Twitter as a Social PR strategist, I received a frantic call from Sarah Van Elzen. As I was driving to my daughter's school to pick her up, Sarah gave me terrible news that one of my employees had just told a blogger to "F*** off" on Twitter. That blogger had, in turn, posted a story about The Buyer Group's PR tactics, and also called out one of my clients.

If you searched our company name on Google, the story was on the first page of search results within 24 hours. I immediately contacted the blogger and apologized for my employee's online behavior and poor choice of actions. I then assured her it was not part of our agency's best practices to act like that in person, let alone on a social media platform. The blogger went on to write a follow-up story at how impressed she was with how professionally the situation was handled, with immediate attention and responsibility for the issue. This new story trumped the negative story on Google. Unbelievably, it all happened within 24 hours.

The lines between social media and PR may at times be blurred, yet they become crystal clear once you realize the potential impact of a single social interaction. Social media has the power to make or break a brand in 140 characters—or in one compromising photo or scandalous video you thought no one would ever see.

PR Peace, Love, and Social Media

The day an employee told an influential blogger to f*** off was one of the worst days of my professional life. However, here I am, touting social media as a great tool for increasing both search and social visibility. That experience actually turned into a case study for my SES panel presentation when I was invited to speak on how to use Twitter for PR at SES New York the following year. CMO's jaws dropped and people gasped or even cringed when I told the story, yet it was a huge lesson to take back to their organizations. We all learned a valuable lesson on proactive communication and facing potential PR disasters surfacing in social head-on.

Duluth

Thanks to Marty Weintraub, globetrotting speaker, author of *Killer Facebook Ads: Mastering Cutting-Edge Facebook Advertising Techniques*, and president of the aimClear online marketing agency, I made my third trip to Duluth in 2013 alongside 30 other search and social marketing thought leaders. Marty and I began chatting in the speaker room at a 2010 Pubcon conference and before I knew it, I'd been booked on a flight to Duluth in the middle of January. My task was to work with the aimClear team on putting together content for the now famous aimClear Intensive Facebook Marketing Workshop, a full day of educational Facebook content for marketers.

I spent 2011 on the road traveling with the aimClear team to SMX West, SMX Advanced, and SMX East, offering up the latest to marketers looking for insider guidance on the nuances of Facebook. Sitting through those full day sessions, I realized how Facebook Ads could help amplify the reach of company news content using the Facebook targeting tools to promote posts.

Social PR Secret:
Leverage the power of Facebook Ads to promote posts to the newsfeed and generate publicity using a blend of organic and paid social PR.

You Say You Want a Revolution

There's so much chatter in the social media and PR worlds. A myriad of people of varying skill sets and areas of expertise have all laid claim to the "social media expert" title, yet what credentials does a social media expert have? PR experts typically have a four-year degree and accreditation. However, PR is a very cluttered and fragmented world right now with the influx of social and the rising influence of search. It's become more challenging than ever to decipher not only what is important to your brand and which tactics to employ, but how to do it and who to trust to manage it. There's no shortage of books that cover the case studies and theory of it all, and many professionals talk a *big* talk.

Yet, when it comes time to deliver, the smoke and mirrors come to light. Not everyone knows everything; I know I learn something new each day. I could easily focus my business on 100% educational training and forget implementation, but I believe in being exposed on the front lines, seeing firsthand how technologies and tactics integrate in order to make public relations better.

We All Want to Change the World

The paradigm shift in the media world has been dramatic and extreme in its scope. Print is shrinking, digital is expanding, and data is exploding. The evolution and revolution of PR happens in shorter spurts and higher jumps. Try to visualize the evolution of PR in icons. It would look like a mash of typewriters, newspapers, televisions, phones, fax machines, email inboxes, chat rooms, Facebook, Twitter, LinkedIn, YouTube, Google, Skype, chat, iPhones, iPads, apps, and infographics. Publicity can change your brand's world in a day—for better or for worse. Landing that *one* story in *The Wall Street Journal,* making the list as one of Oprah's favorites, or tweeting out of the wrong account and ending up the trending topic on *Today* are all possibilities now.

We'd All Love to See the Plan

Talk is cheap, life is short, and PR plans are made to be broken. I've learned a great deal from the practical experience of working through big PR failures and small social media mistakes. Having a plan is important, but more critical is entrepreneur-like agility and the impetus to move quickly and take action. We need flexibility, especially when it comes to building a PR plan that integrates the unpredictable nature of daily news. In the social PR world, today's news is your news; it's what you make of it and how you embed your brand in it. So, what does the social PR plan look like and how do we get started?

Spin It Forward

The rest of this book takes you on a practical tour of today's social PR secrets. You'll work your way through an organized set of chapters on inspiring ways you can do it yourself, impress your clients or boss, and optimize the relationship between social and PR. Here we go!

Chapter 3
Today's Media Relations

When Suzanne Somers started researching expert sources for her *New York Times* bestseller *Ageless: The Naked Truth About Bioidentical Hormones*, she started with a Google search using the keywords "bioidentical hormone therapy doctors." What came to the top page of her Google search was one of the press releases announcing the opening of my client Dr. Paul Savage's hormone therapy practice in Chicago. As a result, Dr. Savage landed a phone interview with Suzanne and contributed a full chapter to her book. Welcome to the new media relations! Getting social with PR, and media relations, starts with getting your brand's news optimized with the search engines.

The primary methods of media relations used to be phone, fax, email, mailing, in-person interview, or a trade show conference. Today, all the mixing and mingling happens online via search and social. An even larger shift with media is the new opportunity for each media person to brand themselves individually. Social media news networks can offer a direct line to mainstream media and, in many ways, can help secure major stories and/or influential coverage.

The Search and Social Media Opportunity

The vast majority of today's journalists use search engines such as Google and social media networks as a story research tool to either begin, confirm, or fact check stories. With that in mind, it's advantageous to optimize your news stories with keywords, tags, and links so the media can find you when researching on search and social.

Getting Social with the Media

- Identify the social networks for your target media: Where are they hanging out and what are they talking about or interested in?

- Follow them and spark up an online conversation.

- Interact and even collaborate with the media.

- Share their stories.

- Leave comments on stories and blogs.

- Update all your media lists with the social networks IDs.

Social PR Secret:
Create a social media list dashboard using a platform such as Tweetdeck or Hootsuite that enables you to see at a glance the social news stream of what is happening with the media you follow.

Social PR and Media Relation Sources

- *Newsle*: When my friends on social media make the news, Newsle lets me know. Newsle tracks friends and alerts you when they're mentioned in news articles or blog posts.

- *PitchEngine*: More than modernizing the press release,

PitchEngine continues to make it easier to get the word out in a social pitch to not just the media, but also your customers. PitchEngine combines the best of the social, visual, video, and mobile worlds.

- *HARO (Help a Reporter Out)*: Reverse it! Brands can use HARO not just to be in the daily know of journalists looking for story sources, but also to research case studies, produce white papers, and create infographics for them to easily use.

- *MuckRack*: Social PR pros understand that Twitter is a tool and not a toy. MuckRack is where journalists and sources connect. Find, follow, and send spam-free pitches to journalists you need to know.

- *Inkybee*: for blogger outreach. aaa(waiting for fix)

- *Buzzstream*: Social, PR and SEO management, a web-based platform that helps build authentic relationships with word-of-mouth influencers across the social web.

- *Toolsy.com*: The best social PR and marketing tools curated for you.

Twitter Chats

Twitter chats are interactive conversations that happen on Twitter with a group of people all using the same hashtag and a certain topic. To take a deeper dive into the Social PR industry, follow some of these Twitter chats, discover your own, or start one for your industry or brand.

TwitterChats* to make your social PR day:

- Sundays: #BlogChat 9 pm ET

- Mondays: #Journchat 8 p.m. ET; #SocialChat 9 p.m. ET

- Tuesdays: #PPCchat 12 p.m. ET; #SocialCafe 9 p.m. ET #GetRealChat 9 pm ET

- Wednesdays: #BrandChat 11 am ET #WJChat 8 p.m. ET #PinChat 9 p.m. ET

- Thursdays: #MyBlogGuest 11 a.m. ET; #SEOchat at 1 p.m. ET

- Fridays: #BusinessFuel 1 p.m. ET

- Saturdays: Take the day off and try a #yoga class!

* Please check your local Twitter listing, programming times subject to change or cancel without a tweet notice.

#Hashtags and Media Relations

A hashtag is a word or phrase prefixed with the symbol #. It's a form of metadata tag. Short messages on social networking services such as Twitter, Pinterest, and Facebook are indexed when hashtags are used to group messages together.

- *Hashtracking.com*: For your social PR intelligence to get the full story, this is a "go-to" source when looking for event insights, news trends, and meme tracking.

- *Social Mention*: It works like Google Alerts for social media, hashtags, and more.

- *Rite Tag*: This helps you reach beyond your followers with the right social optimization tags.

Immediate Response Needed or You Lose

We have 36% less journalists than we had 10 years ago due to budget cuts and print media downsizing. Today's journalist (or blogger) is overworked, underpaid, and typically writing stories on borrowed time and tight deadlines. Over the past few years,

I've jumped the fence over from PR to journalism and can completely relate to being on deadline. News moves fast whether it's an evergreen story or breaking headlines. It seems like no matter what story I'm working on, I need immediate responses from sources or I have no choice but to move on to the next source or idea.

Social PR Secret:

Add social PR live chat to your company newsroom or home page so that a journalist—or anyone, for that matter—can get an immediate response while working on a story deadline.

Recently, I was writing a story and wanted to quote Krista Neher, CEO of Boot Camp Digital, and a leading authority on social media and Internet marketing. I went to her website and saw her company offered a live chat on the website's media area and home page. Even though I know Krista, I needed to get some answers right away because I was on deadline. I typed my query into the live chat box and was able to get my answers with immediate response in a very social and visual way. Think about live chat as part of your website's PR strategy.

Social PR Secret:

"PSA for the world's PR people: Please stop calling me. Email pitches instead. If you don't hear back from me, I'm probably not interested."– Tweeted by New York Times reporter Catherine Rampell (@crampell)

Chapter 4
The New Press Release

Today's press release is lighter, prettier, faster, and more than digital—it's electric news sparked by social media. It happens in real-time, in 140 characters or video from Vine or Instagram, and often bypasses traditional news outlets, originating instead from citizen journalists or inside brands.

Yesterday's static PR news was overweight—delivered in the form of a printed 400+ word press release or a press kit filled with press clippings, photos, DVDs, and brochures and written with the journalist in mind. Today's press release is the opposite of static. It's less, it's more, it's social, it's collaborative, it's fluid, and it's more visual and viral than ever.

Is the press release dead? I say it's evolving as part of this social PR revolution in which we find ourselves. Company news, brand experiences, and community engagement are morphing into the story. Journalists have an abundance of sources from which to gather information, but if you're on the frontline of social PR news content—whether a small business, large brand, or agency side—it's your job to influence the newsmakers and, as a brand, be your own newsmaker using today's evolution of a press release.

In his keynote address at the Zenith Conference, Moz (formally known as SEOmoz) CEO Rand Fishkin stated, "The smartest brands will think and act like publishers."

With that in mind, the "monthly press release" has now morphed into many daily editorialized stories happening direct from the brand and shared by brand advocates. Press releases can be counted in all shapes and sizes of newsworthy content published from a brand's:

- Website

- Website's company newsroom

- Corporate blog

- Social media news channels (e.g., Facebook Page, Twitter stream, YouTube channel, etc.)

- Mobile apps

- Mobile news

- Curated news publishing platforms (e.g., Paper.li, Scoop.it, and RebelMouse, etc.)

In social PR, today's version of the press release is not always published by the brand. A brand's community can break news for the brand, on behalf of the brand, and faster than the brand. Companies like Whole Foods and AG Jeans let the brand's community announce news, too, whether it's what beer is on tap today at the Whole Foods Beer & Wine Bar or what jeans just came in. By snapping visuals on Instagram or pinning ideas on Pinterest, the brand's community is reporting the news for us in many ways.

But, there's still a place for the company press release—the process is shorter, there are more versions, and it's optimized for search and social.

Secrets to Writing Today's Press Releases

Today's successful social PR pros will find it is critical to not only be a good writer, but to also understand the basics of SEO writing. I suggest stepping out of the PR industry to find an educational source within the online marketing industry. Some of my favorite educational SEO and content optimization sources with quality resources, instructors and platforms include:

- SES

- SEMPO

- ClickZ Academy

- PubCon

- SMX

- Online Marketing Institute OMI

- University of San Francisco Online

- Bruce Clay, Inc

- SEOCopywriting.com

- Instant E-Training

- Joe Laratro's SEO Diet

- Copyblogger

- Scribe

Social PR Secret:

Go beyond reading an article on SEO writing; get certified and add some credentials to your social PR life.

Take your social PR results to the next level and become proficient in writing quality titles, meta descriptions, and using natural links and keywords for all of your PR content. Your frequency of social PR content is paramount, just like frequency and timing of a magazine or newspaper. Wouldn't it be odd if *The Wall Street Journal* decided to skip a day? Plan for a news release or news content frequency of at least once a month and ideally two times a month, or, better yet, weekly. It is getting to the point where brands, if they are not already, will be publishing news content daily.

Social PR Secret:
Write three versions of a company press release: one for paid distribution version that includes a photo, logo, and video; another version for the company blog which might be shorter, a little more casual and have a different visual; and a website version that varies slightly from the paid and blog version. This will help index more content with search and avoid possible duplicate content issues.

Visuals can make or break a story from getting shared or republished by top tier media. Match an image—and if possible a video—with each press release, news release, article, or blog post. Studies show that including images and videos with a press release increases page views and search visibility, as well as increasing your chances of getting picked up by a journalist. If you can provide links to videos and embed pictures in a press release, it increases engagement by about 18% for photos and 55% for videos.

Social PR Secret:
Break the press release up into five to ten newsworthy Tweets with a link to the story on the corporate blog or company newsroom. This will send quality referring traffic to the full story.

In social PR, less is more and visual is best. Create a Facebook version of your news that is 100 characters or less with a strong image and a link back to the full story on your blog or website's newsroom or media coverage. Make it pin-worthy! Even if you are not on Pinterest or Instagram, there is a good chance many of your customers are. Let them do the pinning or liking and sharing for you of your news. Without a strong inspiring visual to represent your story, the chances of your story or news getting pinned on Pinterest or noticed on Instagram become slim to none.

PDFs are great for many things, but not for press releases on your website. Don't post press releases or articles on your website in PDF format, as this does very little for you in getting found by search engines like Google, which in turn reduces your chances of the media or your future customers finding you. All news and articles should be in HTML text format and optimized.

Check out press release publishing alternatives to share your news. Publish brand centric or industry news, promotions, and more to new distribution platforms such as PitchEngine, Haiku Deck, or RebelMouse and bring your news content alive in the hands of your moving mobile market or fast-paced newsfeeds.

Social PR Secret:

Pay attention to the types of links in a press release and make sure they follow Google's best practices and recent 2013 changes. For example, over optimized and anchor text links are a big SEO no-no.

In today's content-fueled world, brands are moving far beyond hiring agencies to create ads and launch PR campaigns. Instead, we must venture to create newsworthy and authentic content— videos, blog posts, articles, apps, quizzes, games, and other compelling digital content—built for news discovery and sharing. PR with compelling content is the future, and it means the job as a publicist will become a lot more like that of a reporter, editor, or publisher and less like a "flacker." Today's social PR professional must create newsworthy and brand-centric content beyond the press that gets discovered by the right audience, captures attention, and compels people to share it.

Chapter 5
Content Strategy

First let's get one thing straight in regards to content: It's about *them*, not you. Once you understand that, you can read on.

What makes public relations such a power boost for social media and online marketing? PR secretly spells C-O-N-T-E-N-T, the kind of newsworthy content that Google loves and social media network users will share, like, pin, and follow.

Having a Journalistic Content Strategy

Early in my career, I was the first employee hired in the PR firm Boardroom Communications, which is now one of the leading PR firms in Florida. Julie Talenfeld, prior to launching into Boardroom Communications, was a TV reporter. I learned many things from Julie, but one of the most valuable things I learned was to write like a reporter and less like a marketer.

Julie was—and still is—always looking for the newsworthy angle, the story that will gravitate to the audience instead of build the ego of the client. Today's smart brands are taking a closer look at the quality, delivery, and channels of content and mirroring many of the traditional publishers' best practices: setting themes for days, creating special sections, stepping outside the brand's box, and including non-branded but relative content.

It's Not Me, Me, Me Anymore

PR used to be all about the "me, me, me" of a brand.

"Look at what we are doing and why it's so great. See who we just hired and why they're fantastic. We just announced a new product. We have a new partner who we think is important."

Who cares besides the brand? Really? Social media and self-published company news blogs allow the brand to take a positive editorial step outside the content box and offer up relative newsworthy content that supports the brand, but isn't always talking about the brand.

"Humans are seeking solutions to a problem", explains one of my friends and Million Dollar Websites author, e-business, social media, search and marketing expert Rebecca Murtagh. "Relevance is key. Framing communications in the context of how the new solution solves a specific problem can greatly enhance the value of the story. Proactively addressing key topics for target audiences (media, customers, investors, etc.) goes a long way in cultivating interest, whether you write one general, or three separate press releases.

Social PR Secret:
"And, I cannot stress this enough; always, always, always post a press release on your website first, before submitting to the "wires" to maximize authorship benefits and authority in the discussion—which also enhance visibility in search," says Murtagh.

Examples of Social PR-Friendly Content

- *Well-Written Blog Posts*: Often, blogs are considered the nucleus of a social PR content strategy and can be a vital resource for customers, prospects, the media, and search engines.

- *Expert Guest Blog Posts*: They are a way of getting publicity in another publication. By writing a guest blog post, you position your brand as an expert source on another domain. Looking for guest bloggers for a blog post? Check out MyBlogGuest.com, a community by famed blogger Ann Smarty.

- *How-To Guides*: Use how-to guides as a social PR content strategy to show your audience how to learn something new, offering step-by-step tips.

- *Visuals*: With strong and powerful pictures, illustrations, and graphics, you better amplify your message, explain an idea, and gain user attention.

- *Infographics*: The infographic is one of the fastest growing forms of content marketing, and is an excellent alternative to explaining a complicated subject. Just avoid using them with mobile.

- *Video*: Adding video to a press release, blog post, Facebook, Twitter, or LinkedIn post increases the chance of a story pick, website/blog visits, and more page views.

- *Illustrations*: Deliver news with a visual punch! Spending some money on illustrations to help report your news is a worthy investment. A humorous cartoon or a colorful abstract can go a long way.

- *Testimonials*: Let your happy customers share their stories. They serve as excellent social proof, third party credibility, and a boost to your social search results.

- *Case Studies*: This doesn't have to be an elaborate process; it can be a simple one-pager based on a template of information or it can be customized and include a mix of multimedia and research.

- *Memes*: Pronounced "meem," it means something embraced,

imitated, and shared by the online community as a whole. Memes are typically intended to make people laugh.

- *Email Newsletters*: This is old school meets new school. Email is still a leader in digital communications and journalists still favor email for pitches. Use email newsletters to round up news stories from your own blog, newsroom, and other third party sources.

- *eBooks*: If you've been writing a blog for a few years and have a pile of archives with relevant content, consider repurposing them into an ebook and use it as a point of conversion.

- *Social Promotions*: Sweepstakes, photo contests, surveys, and giveaways are paths to engagement and publicity generators. Check out platforms such as Wildfire by Google, North Social, WooBox, Heyo, and Rafflecopter, just to name a few.

Four steps to an effective social PR content strategy include:

1. Pick newsworthy topics and themes.

2. Write, create, and optimize, being sure to use keywords, hashtags, and Google's best practices in linking strategies. Check out ScribeContent.com, a content optimization platform for smarter content creation, social sharing, and search engine visibility.

3. Publicize and share.

4. Follow KPIs.

Social PR Secret:

Angie Schottmuller, an interactive Jedi, e-commerce expert, and multi-channel strategist came up with the triangle of relevance content strategy that matches perfectly with social PR.

- *Business Interest*: The products, services, company mission, goals, or people relevant to the business or organization.

- *User Interest*: The goals, aspirations, pet peeves, turn-ons, values, hobbies, favorites, values, etc. of your target audience.

- *Time Significance*: Seasons, weather, holidays, life events (birthdays, anniversaries, etc.), major sporting events, current events, trending news and more. Present urgency, popularity, or seasonality. Why is this content relevant now?

> *"You can create the very best content in the world, but if no one can find it, then you've simply not succeeded. Digital PR is a heady mix between creating content and then optimizing it so that your audience can find it quickly and easily."*
> — Danny Whatmough, Director of Digital Strategies at EML Wildfire and Chair of the PRCA Digital Group

Once the type of content, timing, social media outlets, and PR media outlets are figured out, the next step is the social PR editorial calendar.

Chapter 6
Editorial Calendar

Traditional print publishers have used trusted editorial calendars in some form for centuries to manage the publication of books, magazines, and newspapers. PR pros have also been using editorial calendars as a source when trying to pitch client stories to journalists and get stories placed. That was then, but this is now. Social media has dramatically increased a brand's number of owned media outlets, so smart businesses need to make the mental shift to think more like publishers. Managing content with an editorial calendar is a necessity.

While January might be the freshest time to fine tune social PR planning habits, there's no time like now—as in today. One good place to start mapping out a schedule is the social PR editorial calendar.

Remember that file you started last year and haven't opened since? On the flipside, it could be a daily editorial master plan that you *did* follow that made your analytics go through the success roof. In the latter case, maybe it's a do-over or just a yearly update.

The Power of the Written Word

How can the power of the written word impact your social media and PR editorial calendar? Research shows that people who write down goals, share that information with a friend, and send weekly updates to that friend are 33% more successful in accomplishing goals than those who merely formulate them.

If you consider your colleagues, subscribers, prospects, clients, and the media as "friends," think about the power of a written and organized social PR editorial calendar.

Today's social PR editorial calendar takes into account web content, company press releases, blogs, and social media news network postings such as Facebook, Twitter, LinkedIn, Google+, Pinterest, Instagram, and YouTube, as well as email marketing plans and PPC advertising should also wrap into traditional marketing campaigns.

Editorial calendars bridge together content and themes for social media, public relations, and beyond:

- Blogs
- Online newsrooms
- Social media network messaging
- Events
- Email campaigns
- Video
- Offers
- Promotions and sweepstakes
- Web pages
- Seasons and Holidays
- PPC

Editorial Calendar Benefits

Social PR editorial calendars create a cohesive layer to a social PR content strategy that bridges the benefits of:

- *Accountability*: Put it in writing. Cloud applications such as Google Docs or Dropbox allow collaboration where everyone can see it, touch it, and live it.

- *Commitment*: If you put a date on it, chances are you'll get it done.

- *Accomplishment*: Checking it off the list feels great and also ties back to accountability.

- *Planning*: Begin with big picture first, starting at the year, then month, then week, and then day.

- *Creativity*: Mapping out the topics first will help free up space for creativity and inspiration.

- *Trends*: Tie in the topics with keyword research and boost the SEO strategy.

- *Measurement*: Watching the results in growth and also what is popular in content via tools such as Google Analytics will give you valuable information for future editorial ideas.

Navah Berg, a social PR marketing junkie, poetically says this on the topic: "I find a lot of PR professionals set a schedule and follow it, sort of like a template; however, they fail to seize unforeseen opportunities like Oreo's newsjacking during the blackout at the Super Bowl that positioned the brand creatively in the forefront of news. In the Social PR world, there is no such thing as a template. News trends in a social media second and we, as social PR pros, must always have our social PR game face on and be ready to play 24/7."

Tips for Creating an Editorial Calendar

Starting a fresh calendar or conducting a social PR makeover for your brand, the editorial calendar is mission critical for success. These tips are designed to inspire and motivate:

- *Set Goals*: Start with baby steps and grow in phases each quarter. For example, in the first three months consider aiming to produce 40 pieces of social PR content total divided into blog posts and social media messages, and then set a goal for the second quarter to increase by 25%. Watch the analytics grow!

- *Frequency and Timing*: Break it down month-by-month, then week-by-week, and then day-by-day, even hour-by-hour depending on your resources and news cycle opportunity.

- *Themes*: Start with the overall brand strategy and choose topics or themes for each month into broad categories that can be broken down into sub-categories. One place to start is holidays, trade shows, seasons, fashion, sports, etc. Another option is to dedicate each month to a different product focus or service of your company and design a collage of content ideas centered around that product or service in the form of videos, tweets, blog posts, and Facebook updates.

- *Share, Play Nice, and Collaborate*: The social PR editorial calendar isn't designed to be a top-secret document. The idea is to share and collaborate across the team of writers, editors, researchers, and also the other departments such as SEO, advertising, public relations, product teams, and the sales team or even outside contractors.

- *Take Inventory*: Social media networks continue to evolve—many changes have occurred even in the past 6 to 12 months. As new social media networks and applications come into play, adjustments need to be made to accommodate these new messaging strategies. This is not an era to set it and forget it.

- *Social Mobile Messaging*: The explosion of tablet computer usage brings new items to the social media editorial calendar for mobile users. Think about bringing in creative mobile messaging strategies such as location-based specials, QR codes, social offers, etc.

- *Connect with Print Campaign*: Connect the dots between print and online and carry over print advertising themes and campaigns into the social PR calendar and vice versa.

Tools for Editorial Calendars

Organizing your editorial calendar is a matter of preference when it comes to format and what works best for your team. While I'm a very visual person, some love to use Excel and others prefer a collaborative platform. Figure out what works best across your team and go from there, fully expecting trial and error before finding the right solution. Consider some of these tools and platforms as a starting point:

- *Microsoft Excel*: This is the trusted standby and go-to solution that can be at least used as a first step in mapping out a strategy. I personally hate Excel, but so many people live and breathe it that it is many times the first step in an editorial calendar planning.

- *Google*: Google makes it easy to set up editorial calendars using Google Calendar, Docs, Notes, etc. and easy to share.

- *WordPress Editorial Calendar Plugin*: This gives the publisher a "bird's eye view" of your content, allowing you to control your long-term strategy. Celebrity copywriting stars such as Chris Brogan and Copyblogger give this plugin their recommendations.

- *HootSuite*: In essence, your social media editorial calendar is your dashboard of content broken down into timelines. HootSuite gives you that same dashboard feel when you break down the content into social networking messages.

- *21 Habit*: So you want to get your social media editorial calendar up and running in 21 days or less? Put yourself to the test with this app designed to help you make or break habits, whether it be marketing or other business and personal goals.

- *Tracky*: Collaborate the effort with your social PR team inside and outside of your organization—everyone one from freelance writers to photographers to your SEO agency to the online marketing department. Collaborating the effort and streamlining efficiencies will help create the best ideas from the most ideas.

- *ContentDJ*: Producing good content is just as important as curating good content. Check out this new kid on the block before your competition does.

- *Editorial Calendar Software by Marketing*.ai: If you are an "in the cloud" type and like online version with color coding that integrates with platforms such as Hupspot and unbounce, this is for you!

- *Buffer*: This can help make your social PR content life easier by allowing you to schedule content, connect multiple accounts, post at the best times and provide analytics to back it up!

Social PR Secret:

The simple application Buffer can be a secret weapon in bringing old blog content and news releases back to life and send new visits to otherwise dead pages.

Reporting on-the-spot news via social media is one way to get the word out. However, having an organized 12-month editorial calendar that divides the year into monthly, weekly, and daily snapshots can take your social PR content to new levels of success.

Social PR Secret:

Working smarter in social media is a tough balance. New platforms like ContentDJ help identify quality content and publish to social media sites and also come packed with social media editorial calendar to help with content publishing.

Chapter 7
Online Newsrooms

Legal blogger and attorney Roy Oppenheim is a partner of South Florida-based Oppenheim Law. He uses an online newsroom as the hub for his firm's news, op-ed pieces, industry reports, blog posts, and social networks. But he also uses it as a way to communicate directly to the media and subscribers when news is posted. In turn, he reaches national and international media subscribers via email with his message and, as a result, gets media coverage in outlets such as *HuffPost Live*, *USA Today*, and *The Real Deal*.

What's in? Online newsrooms. Call it the new "black," the must-have social PR communications tool that today's journalists expect, publicists-turned-content marketers need, and your organization's website checklist.

Online newsrooms have been a staple part of a corporate website's main navigation since the late 1990s—the static days of public relations and brochure-ware websites. However, today the online newsroom can be an organization's social PR secret weapon.

An online newsroom (also known as a pressroom, media room, press center, or media center) is the section within an organization's website domain that contains news related to the brand or its industry. Today's online newsroom is more than just a chronological list of press releases collecting digital dust—it's visited by not only journalists, but also customers and prospects. The online newsroom content is trolled by search engines and shared via social media. Online newsrooms are social, mobile, visual, and optimized as the news hub and one of the most visited sections of a company's website.

Brands have never had more control and options to publish news and be the source of news, content, images, messaging, and it's a fact that rapidly growing demand for online news continues to squeeze the traditional media. The public is demanding and expecting faster news as it happens with more visuals and easier-to-read stories.

Storytelling

Almost 100% of journalists surveyed expect organizations small and large to:

- Have an online newsroom available to the media.

- Provide access to news releases within their online newsroom.

- Find PR or media contact information readily available within an online newsroom.

- Offer the ability to search news archives within an online newsroom.

Content and the Online Newsroom

Considering constant algorithm updates, online newsrooms updated frequently with quality news and content can only be a bonus for a company's branded online visibility.

More than 50% of journalists are visiting an online newsroom once a week and 64% visit one on a monthly basis. Those numbers should motivate company newsmakers to deliver fresh content and package it in an organized and user-friendly way.

Size Does Not Matter

Expertise in a subject comes in all sizes, with 87% of journalists surveyed saying that they visit both large and small-to-medium sized organization's online newsrooms.

Once known as the placeholder for archived press releases, today's online newsroom is the command central for all company news activity and helps level the playing field for small companies to compete with Fortune 100 companies.

Online Newsroom Checklist

Social Media Networks: Use social media to amplify your message! Make your organization's online newsroom your hub that lists all corporate social media networks.

- *Mobile Matters*: Ensure that your online newsroom is available in a mobile format to maximize your reach. Add responsive design to your list or look at a third-party platform!

- *Get Visual!* Let the statistics speak for themselves. Journalists prefer images and multimedia (so do people and search engines). Search results combined with an image have an increased performance and images are the most shared type of messaging on social media. 94% of journalists surveyed said that having photos on an online newsroom is important.

- *Vital Statistics*: It's really surprising how many organizations fail at incorporating the basic facts, background information, history, and milestones into the press center. More advanced content could include industry hot buttons, facts, and figures.

- *Multimedia Image Library*: Include logos, photos, images, videos, presentations, charts, and graphs. Editors, searchers, and search engines love this stuff, especially when optimized with image file names that make sense and using keywords, alt tags (text alternatives to images), correct file format such as JPEG and offer a variety of image sizes!

- *Bios of Key Executives*: List names, titles, and photos of key management, with relative links to social media networks they belong to. Remember to save the file names of the key executive photos with the first and last name versus something generic.

- *RSS Feeds*: Today's searchers are savvy. Give them the opportunity to easily subscribe to your news and take it one step further by dividing news into categories.

- *Contact Information*: Though it sounds obvious, but many times media contact information is missing or hard to find on press releases and online newsrooms. A 2013 online newsroom report by PressFeed states just 10% of Inc. 500 companies have a contact name on the main page of their news content and an incredible 71% have no contact name on their press releases either.

- *Featured News*: Make sure you have a section that lists most recent significant and relative media coverage, highlighting featured news at the top and using thumbnail visuals if possible, listing in reverse chronological order with a link to more detailed coverage.

- *Architecture*: Have the latest headlines showing on the newsroom home page and make sure the newsroom is easy to find on the home page.

- *Update Often*: The newsroom is an obvious place to add content to your website. This will yield fresh content for your visitors and increase your SEO value.

Newsroom Sources

Online newsrooms are many times on the wish lists of corporate communicators, but on the backburner for the development team. If this is the case, there are third-party online newsroom providers that can have your newsroom up and running in 24 hours or less.

- TEKGROUP

- PRESSfeed

- My NewsDesk

- PitchEngine

- Distribution services such as PRNewswire also offer online newsrooms for companies looking to group news in one easy portal for journalists

Social PR Secret:

PDF press releases and all text press releases are OUT, so make sure your press releases are accompanied with a strong visual, such as an image, video, infographic, or chart. This goes for your press releases hosted on your own website's online newsroom.

The publisher, the editor, the producer, the research team, the photographer, and the fact finder—the social publicist wears many hats and must learn new talents in order to stay ahead.

Chapter 8
The Art and Science of Social Publishing

Dan Zarrella will tell you there's a science to social publishing. After all, he's known as the award-winning scientist of social media at HubSpot and the author of three books on the subject. There are formulas, timing, and even linguistic analysis to social publishing. However, when it comes down to it, there is an art to it that sets your brand's content apart and makes you stand out in any newsfeed. It's the color, tone, shade, humor, sarcasm, timing, opinion, and commentary that spells success.

When you signed up for a Facebook Page or Twitter account, a new title came with it: *publisher*. Each social network you or your brand is connected to is like your own social publication. Think of your followers, fans, or friends as your subscribers and the quantity and reach as your circulation. Your most loyal brand advocates are most likely subscribing to all of your social channels.

What did your subscribers sign up for? Constant ads? No. Exclusive giveaways and promotions? Maybe. Quality content? Yes. They are looking for meaningful, newsworthy, inspiring, and remarkable news content tailored to them. And you are their source for what matters in your overlapping world of likes and interests.

The Art and Science of Social PR

- *Keep social news messages short, sweet, and sticky*: On Facebook, the first 90 characters are the most important. On Twitter, keeping the message at less than 120 characters leaves room for the RT and custom comments.

- *Use strong visuals with your social news*: Photography, bright graphics, saturated colors, and memes that stand alone and work as a means to pull the reader in to view the message and ideally click through to a full story on your website or blog.

- *Write like a social news reporter*: Avoid both extremes: on the one hand, gimmicky, sales-esque type of messages or, on the other, boring and plain messages that don't stand a chance in the competitive newsfeed of Facebook, Google+, or the fast moving stream of Twitter.

- *Write for the Retweet, +1, Share, Like, Klout, and Comment*: Facts, stats, tips, reports, studies, and breaking and trending news are good triggers for prompting a share. Ending a post with a question increases a post's impression and reach.

- *Video reporting*: Creating videos and using them to report news is the pinnacle of storytelling. From a social PR angle, videos can be used for a quick report from the CEO, introducing a new product, or a how-to video that's easier to watch than read. A Vine or Instagram video can be created for a second peek at a tradeshow or conference keynote, a behind-the-scenes tour of what happens at a law firm, a snippet of a yoga class, a happy scene at a Whole Foods event, or a quick recap of a conference.

- *Sharing third-party content*: Reporting news with a share brings depth to your social PR reporting. Not every post can be about you, the brand, or a blog post by the brand.

As part of the social PR content strategy, reporting news by sharing other like-minded content brings goodwill and will position you as a news source.

- *Think SEO (search engine optimization)*: Optimizing content for search and social will increase visibility. Tastefully using branded keywords and phrases along with hashtags and tags can give your post a lift. Understand the basics of search and social optimization including keyword search, links, and meta descriptions.

- *Curating the daily news for your community*: Save your community time and be a resourceful means of getting the news and information for your industry. Sarah Evans does a great job at this with her daily Faves + Co email (formally #Commentz) email that gets plugged into her social networks. One of her taglines is "I do the research so you don't have to." Another example is Mashable; they swipe the news and package it back to you in one easy to read email of the top headlines.

- *Pull Social PR Rank with Google Authorship*: Position yourself as an expert source, an authority on a topic and stand out as an author in search results with author rank. If you're writing for your company blog, guest blogging, or contributing to a publication, it's a social PR competitive advantage to tie in your Google Author rank profile. Your Google+ profile picture will often accompany the article. This is great because people have the option to click through to your article, but they may also visit your Google+ page.

- *Join a Google+ Community (or, Even Better, Create One!)*: Socialize, mix, and mingle with a like-minded community and share expertise, questions, answers, and even news! Hangout, Google style.

- *Every Story Becomes a Pin (and a Referring Link)*: Your

news articles, media coverage, blog posts, and videos are all as Pin-worthy as they are newsworthy! Create "Pinteresting" boards centered on different categories of your news and make sure to pin each story to its relative board. Note: Don't forget to optimize the pins and board descriptions with keyword-rich content along with hashtags.

- *Pin-Worthy Images*: The rise of visual social media marketing makes each image selection for a blog post critical and dictates that you must match each press release or media coverage recap in the company online newsroom with an outstanding visual. Your article, blog post, and news release must be accompanied by a pinnable image to get your social PR news shared in the visual network of Pinterest.

- *Keywords*: Did I mention optimization? If you want your content to be found in a search on Facebook, Twitter, LinkedIn, YouTube, Google+, Pinterest, Instagram, etc., then you must include the relative and unique keywords in the news messaging. Here's an example. *Wrong*: "Our awesome pizza is half price for the next hour." *Right*: "La Gondola Chicago style pizza is half price for the next hour at our Ashland location."

- *Hashtags*: When reporting news within the social networks that support hashtags, make sure to include the relative and trending hashtags to boost your potential visibility. For example, if you're at a conference, make sure to use that hashtag, reporting a trending topic or event such as the #grammyawards.

Social PR Secret:

For maximum clicks on Twitter, place your link about 25% of the way through the Tweet (versus at the end). Dan Zarrella found these tweets had a higher CTR (clickthrough rate) as reported in The Science of Marketing.

Chapter 9
Managing A Community

I can promise you this: no two days will ever be the same for a social PR pro turned community manager, and time management will always be an issue.

Do yourself a favor and read Peter Bregman's book, *18 Minutes: Find Your Focus, Master Distraction, and Get the Right Things Done*. I highly recommend it for anyone in the social media and public relations business. The book was a result of a blog post Bregman wrote for the Harvard Business Review that became one of the most popular and most commented posts on the site. That post, "An 18 Minute Plan for Managing Your Day," began with Bregman's humble admission that we can all relate to. Here's my slightly modified version:

"Yesterday started with the best of intentions. I walked into my office with a keen sense of what I wanted to accomplish. I sat down with my laptop and a my daily Starbuck lattes, checked my Facebook, Twitter stream, Google+, and e-mail. Two hours later, after fighting several digital fires, solving other people's PR problems, and dealing with whatever happened to be thrown at me through my social PR world, I could hardly remember what I had set out to accomplish. I'd been ambushed at social media gunpoint. And I thought I knew better..."

Below, I've taken Bregman's principles and applied them to a day in the life of a social PR professional.

The 18-minute Social PR Day

Step 1 (5 Minutes): Your Social PR Morning Minutes: This is your opportunity to plan your social PR for the day. Before turning on your computer or picking up your smartphone, sit down with the to-do list and decide what is happening to make this a successful day. What can you realistically accomplish, whether it's writing a blog post, researching a new Twitter tool, sitting in on a webinar, or getting ready for that next conference? If you have crossed the digital bridge and *must* turn on the screen versus paper, then check social media calendars in your Google Docs and project management in the likes of Basecamp or social collaborative tracks in Tracky.

Step 2 (1 Minute Every Hour): Social Media Refresh and Refocus: Managing your social media time hour-by-hour is both a discipline and a science. Don't let the hours manage you. How many times do you all of a sudden realize you have spent the last 20 minutes reading Twitter updates, surfing Facebook Pages, or reading an article from an email subscription? Set your phone, computer, or watch to ring every hour and start the work listed on your calendar. When you hear the beep, do a social media check-up. Assess your progress and recommit the next hour to getting back on track.

Step 3 (5 Minutes): Your Social Media After Dark: At the end of your day, shut the laptop and review your social PR day. Ask yourself some questions: "How did my social media day go?" "What did I learn today?" "With whom did I interact?" "Did I meet new followers on Twitter that I should send a quick @ reply?" "Was there a nice RT of me I should acknowledge?" "Are there any comments on my blog I should respond to?"

Building and maintaining relationships is critical in social PR and it's easy to forget that it takes just a few minutes to share appreciation, congratulate someone, or offer thanks.

All that seems easy, but here are some tips to add to the 18-minute plan.

- *Social Media Delete*: It's very hard to say no. All of these unscheduled things can rob you from important and strategic social media time. To get the right things done, choosing what to ignore is as important to choosing what to focus on.

- *Schedule the Hardest First*: Bregman emphasizes (but it is really hard to always do) placing the hardest and most important items at the beginning of the day. He also notes the power of the "when" and "where." Studies show that when you schedule an action item with a time and date, the chances of it getting done are far greater than letting it float.

- *Social PR Community Managers Connect with their Community*: Being on the frontlines of your social media news channels can be a cross between a reporter on a breaking news desk and a community hotline. A traditional newsdesk is constantly looking for tips on breaking news to cover and also juggling the daily programming. A community hotline is on the frontlines and never knows what type of question and comments might come up for moderation and advice.

PR professionals wear many hats, including event planner, crisis manager, spokesperson, newsmaker, and more. And, with the influx of social media, they have the right to claim ownership as social media community manager or, at the very least, part-time manager or moderator. Part-time or full-time, there is no time like the right time to pull community management under the social PR umbrella in some way, shape, or form.

After all, when a community fight, blunder, or issue comes up, guess whose problem it becomes? *"Hello, this the Community Manager calling for PR Manager, we have an issue on Facebook..."*

Salesman to the Left

Malcolm Gladwell coined the term "connector" in his book *The Tipping Point: How Little Things Can Make a Big Difference.* Connectors are people who love networking and are all about making change happen through people. Gladwell describes connectors as those people who know many worlds and can link people to networks they did not know existed.

Social PR Secret:
Connectors make savvy Social PR Managers.
Salesman do not.

What Does it Take to Be a Social PR Community Manager?

- The love of sharing and connecting resources.

- The art of listening. Listening is a natural skill. What is your community telling you?

- Empathy: be able to put yourself in the shoes of the person who is talking to you.

- Editorial skills and a reporter mindset: sniffing out the story with a journalistic flair and voice.

- Customer service: superpowers to squash, handle, and acknowledge.

- The ability to be calm, cool, and collected.

- Fast, multitasking madness with organizational skills.

- A sense of humor.

- Judgment: on the frontlines of social PR community management, it's important to be able to call the shots in real-time and make sure they're the right ones.

- Conversation: you need to know how to attract people to you and create actions within your community in an authentic way.

- In touch: being caring and responsive.

- Resourcefulness: thinking outside the box.

- Visual: you could call yourself a "creative director wannabe."

Social PR Secret:

Read The Complete Social Media Community Manager's Guide by Marty Weintraub and Lauren Litwinka. It's not a skinny book, but it'll be your go-to source for all the essential tools and tactics for social PR community management success—and beyond.

Chapter 10
Jump Into Any News Story

Some call it newsjacking—a term made famous by David Meerman Scott in his best selling book, *Newsjacking: How to Inject Your Ideas into a Breaking News Story and Generate Tons of Media Coverage*, where he describes how the traditional PR model of sticking closely to a preset script and campaign timeline no longer works the way it used to. Say hello to social media and real-time news! The idea of newsjacking is to inject your news into what is breaking or trending, making yourself part of the story and generating media coverage for yourself or your organization.

The term newsjack sounds harsh—like hijack or carjack. A nicer way to say it might be "news lift," where news is used to lift a story on your behalf or to your benefit.

There are a variety of situations in which a brand can break into a news story, such as:

- Sensational

- Tragic

- Disaster

- Commercial

- Breaking

- Seasonal

- Sports

- Celebrity

- Political

- Legal

Making sure that your trusted social PR editorial calendar has flexibility and agility is important to be able to take advantage of or adjust your newstream to accommodate relative news.

Write Yourself into Any Story!

This can be done strategically, swiftly, and easily using the publishing platform of your social media news networks. Here's some advice:

- Pay attention to breaking news.

- Understand the keywords being searched in a particular news cycle.

- Produce high-quality, well-researched content that serves a specific demand for information.

- Quickly syndicate your injected news over social networks to be found when other news organizations search for sources.

- Rewrite and edit the titles and meta descriptions like in this post example.

More Secrets

- Comment on a news story in a top tier publication or

industry blog: reporters, editors, and bloggers pay attention to these comments and will look for expert opinions in future stories.

- Comment on the Twitter news from the reporter with an authentic personal note. For example: "I agree," "Great story," or "Interesting and well-written."

- Retweet a story with an opinion or original twist.

- Facebook: you can share a story from *The Wall Street Journal* and customize the title and description to make yourself part of the story and inject your opinion.

- Write an opinion or editorial piece as a guest columnist or blogger commenting on a story.

- What's the best tone? Positive works better than negative or controversial, but controversial or negative works better than neutral according to recent research by Dan Zarrella.

A Few Rules

- Recognize that unlike traditional PR, newsjacking is real-time and fleeting, so your timing is critical.

- Be sure the story is related to your target market or industry.

- Ask for links when working with a blogger, editor, or reporter as an expert source on an opinion of a trending or breaking story.

- Share the story on social and call out the reporter.

- Acknowledge the reporters.

- Content comes first. PR comes second.

- Use social media for quick dissemination and viral spread

Good Sources

- Google Alerts

- Breaking News

- Google Trends

- If This Then That

- Twitter Text Alerts

- Newsle

- CNN Reports

- Topsy

- Mention.net

Trending, but Predictable

Events, campaigns, holidays, or activities that are already planned are an easy option to consider when looking for news to make yourself part of a trending news story. Events such as The Academy Awards, VMAs, Breast Cancer Awareness Month, or your industry's annual surveys and reports work great. Even holidays such as Valentine's Day, Thanksgiving, and Independence Day can trigger bursts of news opportunities. Predictable events such as the Super Bowl can also be perfect for breaking news opportunities such as the infamous blackout and halftime "wardrobe malfunctions."

Breaking News

- Celebrity gossip

- Social media brand blunders

- Verdicts

- Tragedy

- Sports wins or loses

- Political faux pas

Social PR Secret:

Have your team ready and assigned to predictable
large events as your social PR reporters waiting for
that breaking story to newsjack and make it your own.

For example, Oreo has a team of brand executives and social media staff including writers and designers ready to jump on an opportunity to pull social PR rank, and they did with a touchdown of a tweet.

At around 9:00 p.m. on a Sunday night, Oreo tweeted, "Power out? No problem". Since then, it's been retweeted more than 15,000 times (and the same image on Facebook has received more than 21,000 likes and almost 7,000 shares), meaning that the most powerful bit of marketing during the advertising industry's most expensive day may have been free. That's smart social PR.

Chapter 11
Distribution and Amplification

Distributing your company's news has a whole new meaning since the days of messenger services, U.S. mail, fax machines, and old-fashioned wire services. The first press release dates back to 1906 and in 1954, PR Newswire was first to create a system for electronic distribution of news releases. Prior to its establishment, companies issuing press releases to the New York media had to messenger, dictate, or mail each copy of their news releases to the city's daily newspapers and news services.

With the advent of PR Newswire, companies were able to send a single copy of their news release to PR Newswire's newsroom, where it was simultaneously transmitted to the city's major media points. Today digital domains and social networks, websites, blogs, and mobile apps distribute news in algorithmic speed and analytical codes.

Social PR News Distribution Timeline and Highlights

Here's a brief overview of the history of PR news distribution:

- **1950s/1960s**: PR Newswire is the first to create a system to electronically deliver news releases to the New York media. Business Wire starts as a news release service.

- **1970s**: The first email is sent in 1971 and online forums emerged.

- **1980s**: AOL is launched, making the Internet more user-friendly. PR Newswire begins archiving news releases on electronic databases, including NEXIS (now LexisNexis).

- **1990s**: Internet Wire (now Marketwired) is launched as the first Internet-based press release distribution company. Business Wire is the first service of its type to put its clients' news online, launching the company's website, www.businesswire.com. PR Newswire is next to release news directly to consumers via the Web with the launch of www.prnewswire.com. Internet entrepreneur David McInnis starts PRWeb as a free online press release distribution service.

- **2000 - today**: In 2001, PR Newswire issues the first multimedia news release for Touchstone Pictures while promoting the film "Pearl Harbor." PRWeb offers social bookmarking. Social media links are added to press releases. PR Newswire begins with del.icio.us and later adds Digg, Reddit, Newsvine, and StumbleUpon. Business Wire starts adding social media tags to releases.

- **2008**: PitchEngine is founded by Jason Kintzler as an alternative to the traditional press release and push distribution process of wire services and the first PR publishing platform.

- **2012**: Journalism gets sloppy and PR distribution services get a wakeup call. PRweb issues a fraudulent press release announcing Google's purchase of a Wi-Fi provider. The story is picked up by major media outlets, including AP, Reuters, The Next Web, USA Today, MSNBC, and TechCrunch.

- **2013**: PitchEngine introduces Pitch™ Styles, an Instagram-like feature for social PR content creators, and the Embeddable Pitch, powering more than 55,000 brands.

So Today: Storytelling and Publishing

Organizations have a host of choices when it comes to sharing and distributing company news. Brands are equipped with more publishing power than ever before and don't have to rely solely on third party media outlets to post news. Now, they can do it automatically using their own newsroom, blog platform, social media networks, and also a variety of paid and free distribution and amplification services. Today's brands publish news through a blend of social media, search engines, brand advocates, mobile, visual, and traditional media.

News consumption continues its shift to search engines and social media. With that, social PR pros and content marketers double up as today's news editors and newsmakers by using publishing and distribution platforms beyond the press release.

For brands, publishing news to a paid wire service reaching traditional media and search engines is nothing new. But new outlets and platforms are bubbling to the top, offering savvy ways to reach and engage directly with your audience.

Social PR Press Release Distribution Tips

In the old school days of PR, one press release could result in a wide variety of stories in different publications. As times change, new issues come up and the need for rich and fresh content presents a constant challenge.

Rather than push out the same version of a press release to all channels, repurposing one story into several fresh versions can help maximize distribution and avoid a duplicate potential content penalty from Google. A brand's announcement can have the same message, optimized with the same keywords, but have a variety of different versions that can differ in headline, content intro, and the use of multimedia for best results. Get creative and give the same story a different twist.

- *Paid distribution version*: This could be a traditional 400-word news story optimized with a strong visual and video.

- *Website blog version*: This could be a longer version accompanied by an infographic that tells the visual story.

- *Social media version*: Using strong visuals with a call to action and short teasers of the story designed to lead the reader to the full story on the website newsroom or blog will help your company news stand out in the social news feed.

Today's Social PR Distribution Players

Packaging your company's news content for social media publishing and distribution is an effective way to reach your potential brand champions and create brand advocacy. Building rapport and relationships with consumers, businesses, and media who are most likely to not only choose your brand but also advocate it to their friends, family, and coworkers is key to social PR distribution. Social publishing allows you to increase reach and build trusted relationships and brand equity.

There's a win-win when it comes to press releases and content distribution: Press releases can be used to announce great content such as a how-to eBook or storytelling infographic, and press releases are also a form of newsworthy content.

Flowing and distributing your brand's news content through the various social news networks will ultimately generate the most visibility and leads.

Facebook Newsfeed Distribution for PR

Your Facebook page can be an effective way to distribute company news and help drive quality visits from Facebook to your website or blog. Using a strong visual, a short and optimized version of the news story with a link to the full story on your owned media is the first organic step that is free. As a brand with a Facebook page, you are in essence the editor of your company publication called *Your Facebook Page* and your Facebook Likes are the equivalent to your subscribers. Think of your Facebook page as a magazine and your company news content as part of the editorial strategy.

Reporting your company's news content in a Facebook-friendly way is the first step to driving quality visitors to your website or blog. You can also use Facebook's paid distribution with the Facebook Ad Manager to promote page posts along with sponsored stories to help more people see and engage with your news message, while also helping people discover your news through their friends. Explore targeting the media via workplace targeting and getting creative with your messaging and visuals in the newsfeed.

Twitter Distribution for PR

Twitter can be an effective way to reach the media and influential bloggers in your industry using the social network as a means to find and follow story ideas and sources. A simple way to use Twitter is to organically broadcast your company news in an optimized fashion to your followers (and beyond) with hashtags and links back to full stories on your website or newsroom.

Promoted tweets take advantage of the paid side of Twitter, a social PR distribution option allowing you to put your company news in front of the right people by targeting by geography, gender, and interest, further amplifying your news into the hands of the mobile market. You pay only when people click, favorite, reply, or retweet your news tweet.

Pinterest and Instagram

Use strong visuals to tell your company news stories. Include Pinterest easy sharing options on blogs and use Instagram images and embeddable video option to reach the feverishly growing network.

LinkedIn

Share your news via the world's largest professional network, leveraging a blend of distributing LinkedIn Company Page, Employees, and Groups. Check out the paid side of LinkedIn by targeting media roles in LinkedIn with a combination of general media-related job titles with industry-specific groups.

Google+

Launched in 2011, Google+ is Google's social side and should be taken into consideration as a news distribution option by combining the power of a Google+ Brand Page, Hangouts, YouTube, images, hashtags, and links back to full stories driving traffic back to your blog or website.

PitchEngine

PitchEngine is a modern-day alternative platform for PR news content distribution with publishing perks unlike traditional wire services offering unlimited video, images, sharing. The capability to embed pitches makes sharing press releases and news easy and mobile friendly.

Triberr

If you have a blog with a news feed, try Triberr, a news content distribution and community building platform for bloggers.

Haiku Deck

This offers company storytelling with mobile, social, and visual distribution worth checking out for presentations that are easy to create and a pleasure to watch.

The following traditional PR distribution services target the media, search, and include social services:

- Business Wire

- e-Releases (a personal favorite of mine for value, reach, and ROI)

- Marketwired

- PRWeb

- PR Newswire

Social PR Secret:

Social PR hybrid news content distribution services under the radar include Triberr for news and industry bloggers and Haiku Deck for mobile and visual storytelling and presentations.

Sources:

http://bit.ly/wfcFQI
http://bit.ly/RzfIX

Chapter 12
Mobile and Social PR Hook Up

Studies show the average American has his or her mobile phone within arm's reach 24 hours a day. (Studies by Morgan Stanley) While mixing mobile phones with social media can definitely create a whole new set of crisis-based and reputation management PR services for a publicist or business owner, there's certainly an opportunity to use mobile as a means to deliver news and create positive and proactive publicity for an organization or personal brand.

In the summer of 2012, I started noticing these very inspiring messages popping up on my Instagram feed, all of which were branded with the same black background with a white typewriter style font and all of which were thought-provoking bits of life and business wisdom. The messages were streaming from Sarah Evans' newsfeed and were also being shared on her Facebook page. After about 30 days of mystery messages, the story broke: Sarah was launching a book titled, *[RE]FRAME: Little Inspirations For A Larger Purpose*. Evans describes *[RE]FRAME* as one part personal journey and another part prescriptive steps to help people reconnect to their purpose.

Mobile PR: She Moves in Mysterious Ways

Inspired by Sarah's book launch, here are a few ideas for using mobile for social PR that can be used to cinch some publicity for another product or service launch:

- Use a combination of visual, mobile, and social as a testing ground before a campaign launch. This mini-focus group can quickly give insight as to what resonates with your brand followers and what doesn't. Testing various images, scenes, topics, and more can be extremely valuable and resourceful before launching any product, service, or even content.

- Teasing images and mysterious messaging can get people intrigued as to what all this was leading up to, similar to what movie teasers are designed to do.

- Enroll your audience and create a relationship with them on a topic before you really have something to sell.

- Make sure analytics are in place to measure, assess, and take action. Sarah used SimplyMeasured and Webstagram in her visual and social PR campaign,

Sarah measured which messages scored in data, and only the top ones made the cut for her book.

The Rise of Mobile: It's Here

Taking your company news and publicity mobile isn't on the social PR *maybe* list—it's on the *must* list. In fact, it's on the everyday to-do list. Ask yourself: "How can this message get to the mobile user?" Consider the following when it comes to how mobile is changing our lives and the face of PR:

- 9 out of 10 mobile searches lead to action and over half lead to purchase, according to a Search Engine Land article.

- 70% say they use mobile technologies to follow or monitor

news and information. 51% say they frequently (41.7%) or always (9.2%) share or recommend news from their mobile device, according to a 2012 Mobile News Survey by TEK-GROUP International.

- 30% of time on mobile apps is dominated by social networking, according to HubSpot.

- More than 50% of the leading brands are active on Instagram, according to SimplyMeasured.

Mobile PR 101: Ways to Get Good (or Bad) PR

- *A mobile-friendly website or blog is good Social PR*: If this is not happening yet, you're on your way to be indexed with this hashtag: #FAIL. Have you looked at your brand's website or blog on a mobile device? If it's not mobile-friendly, you could be losing mobile visitors at "hello." Make sure the website or blog loads quickly, is easy to navigate, and offers quick, on-the-spot access to business information such as directions, contact information, and how to easily make a purchase.

- *Watch for changes on Google Local*: Local Google+ pages are unique from other categories of pages because they have features that allow customers to easily connect with that business's physical location. A Google+ page is a free, organic, and editorialized search listing that includes a map of your business's location and features its address, phone number, and hours of operation. Local pages also share the functionality of other Google+ pages, in that you can create and manage circles, start and join hangouts, and share content like posts and photos. You can also connect your Google+ with your YouTube business account and with Google Adwords, so when people click on your ad they +1 it!

- *Read all about it via a mobile-friendly online newsroom*: Make it easy for the media, influencers, bloggers, and customers to learn about your latest news via mobile, especially since 77% say they visit corporate news websites or online newsrooms using their mobile devices.

"It is amazing how many brands are not taking geo-location seriously especially considering the mobile search opportunity," says SEO expert and Pubcon Speaker Liaison Joe Laratro in a Search Engine Watch interview. Laratro offers these mobile PR mistakes to avoid for brands looking to gain mobile search visibility:

- The company's contact information is on the home page but is part of an image, instead of HTML.

- Not including a physical address in the footer and not using schema mark-up.

- Not writing the content of the website in a geo-centric manner.

- Making sure that you claim and regularly monitor your Google+ local/business listing.

Check out your Google Analytics page. See what the mobile traffic looks like and how it is growing. Is your brand ready?

Social PR Secret:
Make your blog mobile-friendly in minutes! If you want a fast and easy way to build a great-looking mobile website in minutes, check out DudaMobile.

Chapter 13
The Rise of Visual Reporting

Heard it through the social PR Vine or an Instagram video news report? That's how brands can break news in today's visual PR world.

"Brands that can rock in visual media will find themselves market leaders," was the closing line of a popular and timely *Fast Company* article by Ekaterina Walter (@ekaterina), Intel's former social media strategist and author of *The Wall Street Journal* bestseller, *Think Like Zuck: The Five Business Secrets of Facebook's Improbably Brilliant CEO Mark Zuckerberg*.

Using strong visuals to tell, sell, and share a story is nothing new. After all, even Traditional Journalism 101 relied on the cover image to sell a newspaper or magazine on the newsstands. Today's cover stories don't just happen by journalists. Instead, visual stories are part of the daily social newsfeed. In PR, offering strong visuals with a press release always seemed to help get your press release to stand out on the editor's desk, but now everyone is a potential editor.

If you think press releases are dead, yours might be because they don't include any visuals. Go check out your past press releases in your newsroom or online. Chances are they didn't include any visuals with the distribution. Imagine posting something in Facebook without a visual; that's almost a misdemeanor!

The Dawn of Visuals Means the Rise of Press Releases

A recent PR Newswire analysis of its press release data revealed that press releases using multimedia assets garner significantly more visibility than text-only releases, up to 9.7 times more visibility.

Social PR Secret:
Adding a strong photo, video, and/or a download-able file to a press release distribution can increase your online visibility by 10 times the views.

That was then, but visuals are now:

- 44% of users (and journalists) say they are more likely to engage with your brand's news posts if the story includes pictures than any other updates. (ROI Research) *That's good PR!*

- 60% of consumers are more likely to consider or contact a business if their images appear in local search results. (Bright Local) *That's good PR!*

- A 37% increase in engagement occurs when Facebook posts include photographs. *That's good PR!*

- 79% of journalists report that images increased the odds of a press release getting picked up. (TEKGROUP) *That's good PR!*

- Readers are four times more likely to engage or comment on a blog post with a good image. *That's good PR!*

- 94% more total views on average are attracted by content containing compelling images than content without images. *That's good PR!*

- 67% of consumers consider clear, detailed images to be very important and carry even more weight than the product information, full description, and customer ratings. *That's good PR!*

Today's company news can happen with a picture, a video, or a Pin and it's social, optimized, and—above all—visual.

Social PR Secret:
Check out Twitter Cards to add visual impact from
your content to Twitter.

Infographic Storytelling Insights

According to Mike Volpe, CMO at HubSpot, a marketing software company, "The best infographics convey a lot of information in a lot less space than it would take to write about the topic or have regular graphs of the data."

Tools and Apps to Make Your Social PR Life Easier

- PicMonkey

- Instaquote

- 123rf.com

- Piktochart

- Infogr.am

- Visual.ly

- Camera+
- Haiku Deck
- Instagram

Visual PR Snapshots of Skills

- Create original images by customizing stock photography with headlines.

- Curate a library of images using Instagram or similar filters and creative cropping.

- Optimize images and videos for search and social with keyword-rich file names, titles, descriptions, and alt tags.

- Learn some simple mobile photography skills, such as lighting, composition, and editing.

- Create inspirational or statistics quotes with typography.

- Use interesting and evoking images with blog posts and press releases. Make it Pin-worthy!

- When launching a new product do not just have the "hero" shot, take photos of the product in use or in application.

- Curate a new library of images using Instagram.

- Take a Pinterest baby step: create a board on Pinterest for blog posts and media coverage.

- Get inspired from other successful brands using visual social media to share, report, and tell their story.

- Optimize your images when using them with blogs and website content to take advantage of Google image search results.

- Borrowing an image? Keep it legal. Get permission first

and make sure you provide a photo credit with a link back. Also, watermark images with your logo to prevent image hijacking.

- Evaluate your online newsroom and make visuals part of your social PR content strategy.

- Don't be afraid to #fail! Try #newthings and #win with #VSMM (Visual Social Media Marketing)!

Social PR Secret:
An excellent infographic is one that not only makes readers say, "This is awesome," it makes them say, "This is awesome...and now I'm gonna share it with everyone I know!"
– Jesse Thomas, founder of Jess3

Sources:

http://bit.ly/Rj0OIv
http://slidesha.re/bgr0uc
http://slidesha.re/ML9fNe
http://bit.ly/14uU4hc
http://bit.ly/JOSyxu

Chapter 14
Scoring Influence

Social PR and influence are like cookies and cream: they go together. By putting them together, you can have a slam dunk in publicity and credibility. Scores do matter, to a certain degree, when it comes to a brand's credibility, visibility, and expertise positioning.

Klout and Kred are among today's most popular social influence reporters. In the real-time world of social integration, authenticity, engagement, and influence do matter and the data is publicly displayed. The question, however, is this: *How much does it matter, and who should really care?* Organizations, brands, the media, and individuals are getting scored, ranked, and labeled on influence.

How Klout Works

The Klout Score measures influence based on your ability to drive action. Every time you or your brand create content or engage, you influence others. The Klout Score uses data from social networks in order to measure:

- *Activity*: The frequency of your social posts and the social actions you take on other people's content.

- *True Reach*: How many people you influence.

- *Amplification*: How much you influence them.

- *Network Impact*: The influence of your network.

- *Content*: Any media that you post to social networks.

How Kred Works

Kred measures influence and outreach in all of your online communities in real-time and

is completely transparent in its scoring system, unlike Klout.

The Kred Score uses data from social networks in order to measure:

- *Activity*: "Generous" actions like engaging with others and spreading their message (re-tweeting or re-sharing).

- *True Reach*: How many people you influence.

- *Network Influence*: You get more points if someone with a large following does something for you.

- *Engagement*: The ability to inspire action from others like re-tweets, replies, or new follows

- *Network Impact*: The influence of your network.

- *Content*: Kred's Community Scores are based on "Influence and Activity" with other people that Kred has assigned to that community.

Ego Power or Social PR Strategy?

Internet marketing experts say brands should pay attention to scoring systems such as Klout and individuals should forget about them. For the social PR professional, that means your brand's social influence score could be a means of evaluating expertise on certain subject. A higher score of influence could be more influential to a reporter, a mark of a clean and credible reputation, and the difference of winning an important media or new business interview opportunity.

Moving Content Through an Engaged Network

Whether Klout, Kred, or influence other players such as PeerIndex, or the offline world, building a social network that delivers a strong ROI has some common foundational elements.

How to Increase Your Social Score on Klout: The Basics

- Build a relevant network.

- Have a compelling content sharing strategy.

- Systematically engage influencers who can push your content virally.

Klout Score Influencers

- Twitter and Facebook carry the most weight.

- LinkedIn and Foursquare don't seem to pull much rank.

- Google+ matters.

- There's some correlation between number of +K's earned and high Klout scores.

- Bing and Instagram are now factored into its social influence measurement tool.

How to Increase Your Score on Kred: The Basics

- Build a relevant network.

- Have a compelling content sharing strategy.

- Systematically engage influencers who can push your content virally.

What Can You Do Right Now?

- Check your social score.

- Scope out your competitor's social score and use this as a competitive analysis opportunity.

- Make sure Klout or Kred topics accurately portrays your brand profile, persona, and expertise influences.

- See how Klout or Kred can fit into your social PR business model. If it makes sense, spend more time with a strategy. If it's not a fit, don't waste time worrying about it.

- Not sure? Try it out for 30 days and see what happens.

- Use these social scores as a means to benchmark if you are trying to monitor improvement or gain competitive insight.

- Use social scores and measurement as a means to research brands and individuals. You can see at a glance what a reporter is engaging in, sharing, and interacting with.

- Don't obsess over it.

How to Improve Your Social PR Score of Influence

- Stay active on your social channels publishing content five to seven days a week. Reminder: social media is more than a full-time job.

- Keep visibility on Facebook, Twitter, and Google+ steady and flowing on a daily basis.

- Stay on top of the favored social network. This seems to be a moving target and brands need to move with it.

- Interact with other influencers.

- Post engaging and electrifying photos with visual impact and messaging.

- Finding more friends and followers leads to a larger network of opportunity.

- Participate in Twitter chats to build reach.

- Stay on topic with content. Content you want to be associated with, that is.

- Optimize your Twitter schedules with tools like Buffer.

"If you want to improve your social influence, a good place to start is by focusing your efforts on becoming more engaging. If you can engage users then you have the ability to influence them. So how do you get people to engage with you? Interact with them and be interesting! Remember, it takes two to tango. The more you engage with other people's content the more likely they'll engage with yours."

— Michelle Marie, social media strategist (https://plus.google.com/u/0/+MichelleMarie/posts) selected by Google as one of the "Most Fun & Interesting" people to follow on Google+ with a placement on Google's elite Suggested User List (SUL) with more than 1.5 million followers on Google+

Who Wins and What's the Score?

Klout's average score is "about 40." Among registered Klout users, a score of 63 puts you in the 95th percentile. A Kred score of 600+ puts a user in the top 21%. A score of 800+ would be top 0.1%. The average score is not published for "Global Kred," but Kred does show the average scores for each "Community" on the Community pages.

So, what's Klout got to do with it? Everything. And nothing.

Social PR Secret:

Social media popularity (in terms of number of friends and followers) does not equate to influence. It's more about having the ability to move content through an engaged network.

Chapter 15
Measurement, Analytics, and Google

Measuring Up to What Matters

How often are you looking at your analytics? Pre-Internet PR was pretty weak when it came down to measurement. The biggest challenge was explaining and defending the value of public relations.

Back in the old PR days, when we first started working on a new account, one of the first things we'd do is start a clipping book (every time a media story came out, it was placed in the clipping book). The thicker, the better. These were one of the main ways to measure how traditional PR tracked media coverage in print or broadcast and it was kept in a "clipping book." What did this equate to in sales and financial terms? The answer: the PR industry turned to advertising media equivalents, so a full-page article would be valued at the equivalent of a one-page ad. Thus, there wasn't a black-and-white way to measure the true value of public relations.

Hello Internet, Search Engines, and Social Networks

Measurement: a big breakthrough in PR and one of the industry's biggest challenges. Today, the data is available to learn what social PR content drives conversions with social audiences, as well as search engines and online media. At the very minimum, every PR professional should have a basic understanding of Google Analytics and access to your brand's Google Analytics account. This is a necessity in today's world, plain and simple. You can find plenty of on online tutorials on YouTube and even via Google, should you need them.

Using data from platforms such as Google Analytics, we can measure the real social PR payoff, validate our services, make better decisions, and gather insights. The amount of measurement and analytics tools can be endless and you can easily spend all day looking at reports and pools of meaningless data, so you need a good plan. Here are a few:

- *Start with the basics first*: It all starts with the basic understanding of your owned properties first, so begin with the web analytics of your owned media: your website and blog first, and then move to looking at other outside data analytics.

- *Measuring in all the right places*: At the end of the day, the most important analytics are what matters most to your business goals. This could be email sign-ups, subscriptions, product sales, media mentions, visits, or shares.

- *Today's social PR KPIs*: Setting key performance indicators (KPIs) prior to a Social PR campaign allows you to set benchmarks to measure against and helps get the "buy in" from all the decision makers. Make sure everyone (from the president to CMO to sales manager to marketing) is on the same page as what the meaning of success looks like. Of course, the ultimate KPI is the actual sale or conversion (financial ROI) or the front-page story in *The Wall Street Journal* (many times ego-ROI), but there's a journey involved in that ultimate KPI win, a process of touchpoints, relationship building, and nurturing.

Social Public Relations Key Performance Indicators Examples:

- *Volume and Depth KPIs*: This could be the quantity of articles or the number of articles that communicate the brand's message.

- *Sentiment KPIs*: Tracking the percentage of positive or negative comments across the social and search graphs.

- *Engagement KPIs*: The number of @mentions, retweets, +1, likes, shares, comments on articles, organic media reactions, etc.

- *Conversion KPIs*: This could be the number of email signups as a result of a news release or number of white papers requested from a webinar.

Whatever the KPIs are, list them and be specific. Football is a great analogy for goals and objectives, so think of your objectives as the yards and downs along the way and the goals as your touchdowns. Make sure to set KPIs so you can keep score!

If you're using social media as a means to get publicity, visibility, and quality exposure, then tuning into Google's Analytics social media reports is vital to success, though this isn't a native skill to many communications professionals.

I can't think of a more perfect person to be a Product Marketing Manager at Google Analytics than Adam Singer. He's extremely passionate about digital marketing and PR, technology and media companies, and anything new that connects us and allows for better communication in our world. We not only share the same social PR enthusiasm, but have also shared a few Social PR conference panels together, spreading the good word about optimizing the PR and marketing process for better conversion. Today, Adam provides guidance through a host of industry webinars, blogs articulating insights on how the PR industry can best use Google's Social Analytics, as well as the publicity factors of a brand using Google+.

Social PR Secret Tips on Measurement

Two main points to measure using Google Analytics are: (1) referring traffic and (2) the full value of traffic coming from social sites and measure how they lead to direct conversions or assist in future conversions.

Social media and PR are typically in the early "dating" part of an organization's relationship building. On average, customers interact with a brand 4.3 times over a two-day period before they finally make a purchase. So, just like in the old days of PR, social media and PR may not get the full credit they deserve for those only looking at last-click attribution.

> Social PR Secret:
> Think beyond the obvious KPIs such as number of followers and quantity of visitors. Instead, think about KPIs such as email sign-ups or newsletter subscribers, types of KPIs that could eventually lead to the ultimate KPI: a new client or customer.

Singer reminds marketers to pay attention to which networks are working best for your brand and adjust accordingly.

Watch the Social Flow via Google Analytics. This report starts with the source of traffic, such as Twitter, and breaks down how many people stayed on the site to visit another page and which pages they visited, basically illustrating how your website visitors that originated from a social network move through your site.

Social PR Secret:
Keep in mind that Google has the largest audience and make sure your brand, organization, or client is set-up properly and active on Google+ and YouTube.

Google+ influences how you look in search results in a visual way and is important from a PR perspective. You always want to own the first page of search and be proactive in the event of negative reviews or a bad online story.

Google+, when properly optimized and managed, can serve as an influence to positive reputation management for a brand.

Social PR Secret:
On Google Analytics, use this custom Google Social dashboard: troni.me/GASocialDas.

- Be active on all the social sites that matter. Research what channels your audience likes best.

- Creating dashboards for the numbers and metrics that matter most will make your social PR life easier and result in better decision-making, budget planning, and account-ability.

Social PR Secret:
Check out Blitzmetrics.com for social analytics dashboards that allow you to monitor beyond Google and across all social media channels and see what social PR content is having the most impact, while also recognizing your brand evangelists.

While many social PR professionals are already measuring—in fact, we're swimming in numbers and reports—the question is: Who is doing this effectively and efficiently? Measuring what matters to the brand's business objectives is all that truly matters at the end of the day.

Social PR Secret:

Looking for a visual way to report Google Analytics? Have Visually Google Analytics Report automatically delivered to your inbox each week. Learn more at: https://create.visual.ly/graphic/google-analytics/.

Check out nitrogr.am, webstagram, and Simply Measured for even more analytics.

Chapter 16
Avoiding a PR Disaster

Does the saying, "There's no such thing as bad publicity" apply to social media blunders gone viral? Your brand ending up as a gag skit on SNL because of a social media mishap is probably not part of your PR strategy.

If you think social media and PR are two different departments with separate agendas, think again. The good, the bad, and the ugly stemming from social media sentiments that bubble up to a brand are a direct reflection on the company's image, credibility, influence, visibility, and—if you're a public company or a company trying to raise money—your investors. In more cases than not, employees behaving badly by accident or intentionally have the formula for PR disaster. Now social media is part of the PR department, and it's their problem.

Zen of a Social Media Policy for Good PR

- *Your employees are social! #FTW or #FAIL*: As the popularity of social media grows, brands small and large must face the fact that the people with the closest connection to your organization—employees—are active on social channels. While employees can be your perfect brand advocates and evangelists, they can also burn your reputation when they lose control on social media networks.

- *The employee social media manual #Trending #HR #PR*: To mitigate that risk, develop a company-wide policy that clearly defines both acceptable and unacceptable behavior on social media, and dictates how employees can effectively communicate your brand culture, voice, and message. Include guidelines about confidential and proprietary information and how each should be treated and balanced against the transparency that consumers increasingly expect from social media.

- *Social media training program #Breaking #Success*: The company picnic and holiday party just got bigger, wider, and riskier with social media snapshots landing on Facebook and Instagram. Is that a shot of tequila that the CEO is doing? Hello front-page news and PR hangover. Planning and determining who will provide your employees with these resources will take the guesswork out of determining what's appropriate to post, tweet, or share. It also increases the consistency of communications about your brand. Consider delivering educational resources to your employees as part of a company-wide social media training program.

A recent report published by the Wildfire Google Team, *The Road to ROI: Building Strategy for Social Marketing Success*, speaks to how to influence the conversation without trying to control it. One of the key areas focused on in the report was the internal planning of social media and how that ties into the external public relations and reputation management of a company.

Your social media policy should specifically address these ten questions:

1. What are the goals of your social media policy?

2. How will you update your policy and reinforce it?

3. What information about your business can employees share?

4. Which social networks will you maintain a presence on?

5. How will you monitor conversations about your brand on social channels? Who, specifically, will monitor these conversations?

6. How will you maintain a consistent social tone and style across these networks?

7. Will you encourage employees to participate in social media as a representative of your brand?

8. How will you respond to consumers who communicate with your brand through social channels? Who will respond on your brand's behalf?

9. Who is authorized to proactively post on your brand's behalf? Does this authorization account for different regions and teams?

10. What constitutes a social media "crisis" for your business? What is your process for handling a post that could be categorized as a crisis?

PR+: Social Media Policy Resources

- Addvocate: According to the recent 2013 Edelman Trust Barometer, employees rank higher in public trust than a company's PR department, CEO, or founder. Begging employees to share, tweet, post, and Like can be exhausting—and let's not even talk about the inefficiencies of wasted time. Addvocate makes it easy to empower, track, and reward your employee brand advocates, making them part of the solution.

- Social Media Policy Tool: When you can't wait for the red tape and need it quick, check out this streamlined process that merely requires you to answer a brief questionnaire and provides you with a complete social media policy customized to your company.

- Social Media Policy Database: Ever wonder what the social media guidelines look like for big brands like Coca-Cola, Nordstrom, or Walmart? Consider it done! This is the most complete listing of social media policies, referenced by the world's largest brands and agencies.

A key takeaway from Wildfire's report is to not treat social media as a silo. One of the biggest hindrances happens when social media is treated as separate category without collaboration and interaction from marketing, PR, and customer service. How does your social media policy measure up?

A portion of this chapter originally appeared in Search Engine Watch.

Chapter 17
Strategy for Tragedy

We interrupt this regularly scheduled program for...

The concept of brands becoming and acting more like editorial publishers is evident, as organizations opt to do what the media is doing, focusing on what's actually happening real-time in the news.

Do we really need to have this conversation? Truthfully, I'd rather not, yet the tragedies such as the Newtown, Connecticut shooting and the Boston Marathon bombings bring a new normal to a day in the life of a social PR professional. As tragedy unfolds, it's now our job to edit our social PR calendars to include the new, embrace the news, or remove our news from the social feed to allow room for what's most important.

When the unthinkable and unpredictable happens, life must still go on. As much as we wish the world could stop for a moment so we could collect our thoughts, business marches on.

I didn't choose to be in crisis management. It chose me when one of my best friends was murdered by a serial killer. I was just starting my career in PR and suddenly found myself, alongside my friend's family, under the spotlight of a tragic national news story. I understand all too well what those families are going through with what can seem like a circus of media.

Everywhere we look in the wake of tragedy, people and organizations struggle to express their acknowledgement or sympathies without crossing the boundaries that could make their messages appear self-serving or selfish. People are, by nature, skeptical of brand messaging.

Behind businesses are real people and as people; we are all affected. The Newtown shooting and Boston bombings raise questions on how a brand should interact with fans during a crisis and the unwritten rules of social media etiquette.

How Can Brands Support Audience on Social Media?

If you're debating the power of social media for PR power, here's more proof that it matters: about 50% percent of consumers think a brand's Facebook page is more useful than a brand's website, a study by Lab42 suggests.

If a brand really wants to have a personal relationship with its audience and be seen as more than just a way to get coupons and giveaways, they need to offer more than promotional content. Brands need to offer resources—that is, meaningful content. The first step is being real and getting personal.

Your brand needs to be real during a community tragedy:

- *Be human*: Acknowledge what's happening.

- *Be real*: Stop automated posts. Get in real-time when tragedy strikes.

- *Be credible*: Report and share news, but confirm sources and facts first.

- *Be caring*: Consider sensitive subject matter. If your brand is part of the tragedy or in a related industry, take a close look at what you're reporting.

- *Be considerate*: Take a few days off from your normal editorial calendar. Think about it—is anyone even paying attention to what you're promoting at that moment?

- "I typically recommend to cease posting branded content for the day, however always remain active in the community (regular moderation responsibilities)," writes social media and PR specialist Lisa Grimm in a heartfelt blog post she published the day of the Newtown shooting.

- *Be alert*: Have a meeting with the communications team and put someone in charge of watching real-time news so you're aware of issues—good or bad—that can impact your community.

- *Have a clean slate*: Consider taking down recent postings that might be offensive to current events.

- *Look at the most recent posts*: Are they appropriate in light of the recent news? I would have deleted these posts or posted something acknowledging the relative of the shootings so that such content was not the most recent post for the first 5 days.

Why Brands Shouldn't Ignore Tragedy

Sadly, I know what it's like to deal with the media surrounding a national story and be the target for interviews. The reason the collective conscience is so affected by tragic events is precisely because so many, if not all, of us have experienced tragedy in our own lives. We can't help but be empathetic. We want to stop the suffering of those affected because we know how damaging it really is. This "we" includes business owners and management, too.

Even if your customers were not directly affected, they certainly empathize with those who were. They may feel helpless, desolate, or even experience survivor's guilt.

According to a recent study, 70% of people get most of their news from friends and family on Facebook and 36% get most of their news links from friends and family on Twitter, with more of the Twitter crowd using a smartphone. If you are putting your content in the social newsfeed during tragedy, think about if it is relevant or just taking up newsfeed space.

You Can't Schedule Life, or Social Media

While scheduling tools are helpful, social media PR news isn't something you can set and forget. These are communities of people who interact in real-time, and if you're lucky enough to have a community grow up around you as a brand, you should be just as plugged in as they are in order to strengthen your relationships and sustain your reputation.

Education and Strategy are Paramount

Let's face it: social media is not always in the hands of accredited PR professionals with years of crisis management experience on their resume. Does your community manager know the answers to these questions?

- Do we comment during a natural disaster or national tragedy? If so, what does doing so look like?

Chances are if they don't, then neither does the organization. Consider having a plan in place to take action such as:

- Cease all scheduled or planned content for a period of time.

- Check ad schedule and pull content promotion or campaigns for a period of time.

Check Your Sources, Even When It's Not a Tragedy

Brands are learning to become news content publishers, and are getting bruised and beat up along the way. The ones who succeed will follow journalism and communications best practices, regardless of the topic by doing routine editorial fact checking and confirming sources.

Social PR Secret:

In a time of tragedy or crisis, check out sources, and be sure to fact check. The last thing you want to do is perpetuate misinformation.

Chapter 18
Social PR Wisdom

In my social PR journey, many people have inspired me along the way. From the best bosses to those who frustrated me to some of the most powerful and passionate CEOs, authors, speakers, clients, friends, mentors, "frenemies," experts, consultants, business coaches, personal trainers, yoga instructors, doctors, journalists, and—most recently—the search marketing and social media industry.

One standout social PR inspiration I encountered early on was Tony Hsieh, CEO of Zappos.com, Inc. and author of *Delivering Happiness: A Path to Profits, Passion, and Purpose*. An early adopter of Twitter, he flocked to social media as a path to share his inspirations, in addition to learning how to cultivate a culture of happiness and success through his wins and losses.

I am happy to share my journals, sticky notes, and excerpts from my social PR life.

Social PR Secret:
"Be passionate, tell personal stories and be real."
– Tony Hsieh, Delivering Happiness.

De-Friend Your Fears

Being in the PR industry during the millennium, dot-com, go-go days was an interesting time, especially with emerging technology startups. Checks were being FedExed to my agency without proposals from companies I'd never spoken to. One of my dot-com clients was a CEO trying to raise money to go public. We were planning media tours and investor road shows with the big shots on Wall Street, Madison Avenue, and Silicon Valley.

One social PR secret I had to keep for my client was the fact he was gay. At the time being *out* was not *in*. It was a different era when the good old boys on Wall Street would not accept homosexuality on a term sheet and might actually blacklist someone for something along those lines. Coming out of the gate and being the "first" to do something or get labeled means risking it all for the reward of someone in the future. Today, same-sex marriage is one of the most talked-about topics on Twitter and in blogs, and being gay on Wall Street is now just a blip on the social radar. Being *authentic* is in.

Today's public is looking to have a transparent and meaningful relationship with brands. These days, it's less about contrived messaging and more about being real, even if real means tripping and getting back up, making mistakes and owning up to it, closing chapters and starting new ones, and sometimes turning everything off and reinventing your brand or yourself from the bottom up. As an example, Madonna is famous for reinventing her persona to match what her fans want.

More has changed in public relations and the media in the past five years than in the past 100 years, so the social PR soul searching is really just beginning.

The Best Seat in the House for Opportunity

I've spent the last few years speaking at leading Internet marketing conferences on the subject matter of social media and SEO as it relates to public relations. Webinars, conferences, workshops, and online training courses are a new way of life for me and I love sharing the perspective of how PR plays into the game. But what I love even more than speaking is the opportunity to attend the other sessions at a conference. I map out my session plan ahead of time and I always sit in the front row with my laptop or iPad, feverishly taking notes. Sitting in the front row gives you an advantage of having less distractions, more focus, and a better networking opportunity because most of the other front-runners are live bloggers or members of the media who are there to cover the session. Some of my best contacts and relationships have either been made sitting in the front row or in the speaker room at a conference.

From #Fail to #Success

Besides staying in the news with a positive angle, part of the daily routine of a social PR professional is to stay ahead of the news, reading all of the relative buzz surrounding your brand's industry and the world events that impact everyone. But, when the cringing moment comes and you read a negative story about your brand, client, or yourself in the media, all the good fades to nausea.

One of my favorite employees who had the ultimate and, of course, authentic British accent, Radley Moss, was called out in a print story by the editor of a Florida business journal. The headline, "Some pitches are in the dirt," called our story idea "Internet hype." Radley brought the article into my office and read it to me. I said, "Call the editor up and ask him to lunch." So, the three of us met for lunch and from that experience, we gained some valuable advice from the editor about how and what to pitch, and the editor also got to hear what life was like on our side of the media fence. It's the failures that make us stronger and give us opportunities to grow and succeed.

These days, with social media, the opportunity to fail is at an all-time high for a publicist of any sort, business or celebrity. One wrong move by anyone within a company ends up in the lap of the PR department.

Keep Moving With the PR Cheese

It would be easy if the same old routines always worked in every situation. In the book, *Who Moved My Cheese: An Amazing Way to Deal With Change in Your Work and in Your Life* by Spencer Johnson, the characters are faced with unexpected change—much like the online marketing, media, and PR industries: dealing with change is like a maze.

> Social PR Secret:
> Once you realize that failing doesn't mean it's the
> end of the world, changing becomes a little easier.

Staying in the same PR routine from five or ten years ago is old cheese. Being flexible, keeping things simple, and giving yourself the green light to move quickly allows you the space to notice that when a situation changes, you should change with it. Social media has caused more than change for PR; it's caused an enormous opportunity shift. The University of Florida College of Journalism now offers an Online Master of Arts in Communication with a specialization in Social Media that is worth checking out.

> Social PR Secret:
> "The only thing you can change is how you
> relate or how you react to something."
> – Chelsea Dipaola, Guruv Yoga instructor

Social publicist and digital strategist Lisa Grimm puts it like this: "Don't accept the structures around you. Pick something small, build something new and get results so you can build more new things."

Social PR Secret:
Don't sit around and think how you can be like other people, brands or companies. Define your own way, your own structure for operating and the creative processes that drive your purpose and objectives.

The new social PR cheese comes full of opportunity. Take a bite, keep moving, and create the space for things to happen.

About the Author

"That's why it's called a practice.
We have to practice a practice if it is to be of value."
— *Allan Lokos,* Patience: The Art of Peaceful Living

When it comes to balancing relationships, Lisa Buyer @lisabuyer believes the practice of public relations, social media, and SEO is exponential. As the founder of three media companies and CEO of The Buyer Group (www.thebuyergroup.com), Lisa is ambitious about the influence of public relations on social media, SEO, and SEM, and she continues to share her innovative approach with her followers, clients, peers, and associates. Heading her current boutique agency, The Buyer Group, Lisa consults on both the client side and agency side.

She writes and tweets for industry publications, Search Engine Watch and ClickZ, and she is the editor of her own online publication, SocialPRChat.com. Lisa is often recognized for her inspirational and motivational style. She is an educator and a frequent speaker at search and social conferences, workshops, and webinars.

Lisa helps clients connect the social media and PR dots while also educating agencies transitioning from traditional media to today's best digital strategies. Past clients include public and private companies in the technology, real estate, and health/beauty industries as well as marketing and advertising agencies.

She is a regular speaker and moderator on topics of online PR, social media, and search at national conferences including SES, SMX, PubCon and MediaPost. She is a graduate of the University of Florida with a degree in Public Relations and Business Administration. (Go Gators!)

Lisa lives in Celebration, Florida, with her family: Don, Kennedy, Audrey and Grant. Besides #SocialPR, Lisa's favorite hashtags include #yoga, #surf, and #sunsets.

"Practice and all is coming." ~ Sri K. Pattabhi Jois

#SocialPRSecrets Twitter List

123rf.com
@123rf
https://twitter.com/123rf

21 Habit
@21habit
https://twitter.com/21habit

Adam Singer
@adamsinger
https://twitter.com/AdamSinger

Addvocate
@addvocate
https://twitter.com/addvocate

AG Jeans
@agjeans
https://twitter.com/AGJeans

aimClear
@aimclear
https://twitter.com/aimclear

Amy Vernon
@amyvernon
https://twitter.com/amyvernon

Angie Schottmuller
@aschottmuller
https://twitter.com/aschottmuller

AP
@ap
https://twitter.com/AP

Blitzmetrics.com
@BlitzMetrics
https://twitter.com/BlitzMetrics

Boot Camp Digital
@bootcampdigital
https://twitter.com/bootcampdigital

Bruce Clay Inc
@BruceClayInc
https://twitter.com/BruceClayInc

Buffer
@bufferapp
https://twitter.com/bufferapp

Business Wire
@businesswire
https://twitter.com/BusinessWire

Buzzstream
@buzzstream
https://twitter.com/buzzstream

Camera+
@taptaptap
https://twitter.com/taptaptap

Catherine Rampell
@crampell
https://twitter.com/crampell

Guruv Yoga
@tymihoward
https://twitter.com/tymihoward

Chris Brogan
@chrisbrogan
https://twitter.com/chrisbrogan

ClickZ Academy
@incisive
https://twitter.com/incisive

CNN
@cnn
https://twitter.com/CNN

ContentDJ
@contentdjapp
https://twitter.com/contentdjapp

CopyBlogger
@copyblogger
https://twitter.com/copyblogger

Dan Zarrella
@danzarrella
https://twitter.com/danzarrella

Dana Todd
@DanaTodd
https://twitter.com/danatodd

Danny Sullivan
@DannySullivan
https://twitter.com/dannysullivan

Danny Whatmough
@dannywhatmough
https://twitter.com/DannyWhatmough

David McInnis
@giantcranberry
https://twitter.com/giantcranberry

Dennis Yu
@dennisyu
https://twitter.com/dennisyu

Digg
@Digg
https://twitter.com/digg

Dr. Paul Savage
@ageology
https://twitter.com/ageology

Dropbox
@dropbox
https://twitter.com/Dropbox

DudaMobile
@dudamobile
https://twitter.com/DudaMobile

e-Releases
@ereleases
https://twitter.com/ereleases

Edelman Trust Barometer
@edelmanpr
https://twitter.com/edelmanpr

Ekaterina Walter
@ekaterina
https://twitter.com/ekaterina

Facebook
@Facebook
https://twitter.com/facebook

Fast Company
@FastCompany
https://twitter.com/FastCompany

GetRealChat
@PamMktgNut
https://twitter.com/PamMktgNut

Google
@Google
https://twitter.com/google

Greg Jarboe
@gregjarboe
https://twitter.com/gregjarboe

Gneo Day
@gneoday
https://twitter.com/gneoday

Haiku Deck
@HaikuDeck
https://twitter.com/HaikuDeck

HARO
@haro
https://twitter.com/helpareporter

Hashtracking.com
@hashtracking
https://twitter.com/Hashtracking

Heidi Cohen
@heidicohen
https://twitter.com/heidicohen

Heyo
@heyo
https://twitter.com/heyo

Hootsuite
@hootsuite
https://twitter.com/hootsuite

HubSpot
@hubspot
https://twitter.com/HubSpot

Huffpost Live
@huffpostlive
https://twitter.com/HuffPostLive

If This Then That
@IFTT
https://twitter.com/IFTTT

Infogr.am
@infogram
https://twitter.com/infogram

Inkybee
@forthmetrics
https://twitter.com/forthmetrics

Instagram
@instagram
https://twitter.com/instagram

Instant E-Training
@IETraining
https://twitter.com/IETraining

Instaquote
@getinstaquote
https://twitter.com/getinstaquote

Jason Kintzler
@jasonkintzler
https://twitter.com/jasonkintzler

Jesse Thomas
@jessethomas
https://twitter.com/jessethomas

JETLAUNCH
@jetlaunchllc
https://twitter.com/jetlaunchllc

Joanna Lord
@JoannaLord
https://twitter.com/JoannaLord

Joe Laratro
@jlaratro
https://twitter.com/jlaratro

Julie Talenfield
@boardroompr
https://twitter.com/boardroompr

Klout
@klout
https://twitter.com/klout

Kred
@kred
https://twitter.com/Kred

Krista Neher
@kristaneher
https://twitter.com/KristaNeher

La Gondola Chicago
@lagondola
https://twitter.com/LaGondola

Lab42
@Lab42Research
https://twitter.com/Lab42Research

Lauren Litwinka
@beebow
https://twitter.com/beebow

Lee Odden
@leeodden
https://twitter.com/leeodden

Lisa Grimm
@lulugrimm
https://twitter.com/lulugrimm

Malcolm Gladwell
@gladwell
https://twitter.com/Gladwell

Mark Zuckerberg
@facebook
https://twitter.com/facebook

Marketwire
@marketwire
https://twitter.com/marketwire

Marty Weintrub
@aimclear
https://twitter.com/aimclear

Mashable
@mashable
https://twitter.com/mashable

Matt McGowan
@matt_mcgowan
https://twitter.com/matt_mcgowan

Melanie Mitchell
@MelanieMitchell
https://twitter.com/MelanieMitchell

Mel Carson
@melcarson
https://twitter.com/melcarson

mention
@mention
https://twitter.com/mention

Michell Marie
@imizze
https://twitter.com/imizze

Mike Volp
@mvolpe
https://twitter.com/mvolpe

Moz
@Moz
https://twitter.com/Moz

MSNBC
@MSNBC
https://twitter.com/msnbc

MuckRack
@muckrack
https://twitter.com/muckrack

My News Desk
@mynewsdesk
https://twitter.com/mynewsdesk

MyBlogGuest
@myblogguest
https://twitter.com/myblogguest

MySpace
@myspace
https://twitter.com/Myspace

Navah Berg
@Navahk
https://twitter.com/navahk

New York Times
@nytimes
https://twitter.com/nytimes

Newsle
@newsle
https://twitter.com/newsle

Nitrogram
@nitrogram
https://twitter.com/nitrogram

Nordstrom
@nordstrom
https://twitter.com/nordstrom

North Social
@NorthSocial
https://twitter.com/NorthSocial

Online Marketing Institute
@OMInstitute
https://twitter.com/OMInstitute

Paper.li
@smallrivers
https://twitter.com/SmallRivers

PeerIndex
@PeerIndex
https://twitter.com/PeerIndex

Peter Bregman
@peterbregman
https://twitter.com/peterbregman

PicMonkey
@pikmonkeyapp
https://twitter.com/PicMonkeyApp

PiktoChart
@piktochart
https://twitter.com/piktochart

Pinterest
@pinterest
https://twitter.com/pinterest

PitchEngine
@pitchengine
https://twitter.com/pitchengine

Pluggio
@pluggio
https://twitter.com/pluggio

PressFeed
@pressfeed
https://twitter.com/PRESSfeed

PRNewswire
@prnewswire
https://twitter.com/PRNewswire

PRWeb
@PRWeb
https://twitter.com/prweb

Pubcon
@pubcon
https://twitter.com/pubcon

Rafflecopter
@Rafflecopter
https://twitter.com/rafflecopter

Rand Fishkin
@randfish
https://twitter.com/randfish

Rebecca Murtagh
@virtualmarketer
https://twitter.com/virtualmarketer

RebelMouse
@rebelmouse
https://twitter.com/rebelmouse

Reddit
@reddit
https://twitter.com/reddit

Reuters
@Reuters
https://twitter.com/Reuters

Rite Tag
@RiteTag
https://twitter.com/RiteTag

Roy Oppenheim
@oplaw
https://twitter.com/OPlaw

Sarah Evans
@prsarahevans
https://twitter.com/prsarahevans

Sarah Van Elzen
@SarahVanElzen
https://twitter.com/SarahVanElzen

Scoop It
@scoopit
https://twitter.com/scoopit

Scribe
@ScribeContent
https://twitter.com/ScribeContent

Search Engine Watch
@sewatch
https://twitter.com/sewatch

SEMPO
@sempoglobal
https://twitter.com/sempoglobal

SES
@sesconf
https://twitter.com/sesconf

SimplyMeasured
@simplymeasured
https://twitter.com/simplymeasured

Slimbooks
@slimbooks
https://twitter.com/slimbooks

SMX
@smx
https://twitter.com/smx

Social Mention
@socialmention
https://twitter.com/socialmention

Starbucks
@starbucks
https://twitter.com/starbucks

StumbleUpon
@stumbleupon
https://twitter.com/StumbleUpon

Suzanne Somers
@SuzanneSomers
https://twitter.com/SuzanneSomers

TechCrunch
@techcrunch
https://twitter.com/TechCrunch

TEKGroup
@tekgroup
https://twitter.com/TEKGROUP

The Buyer Group
@thebuyergroup
https://twitter.com/thebuyergroup

The Next Web
@TheNextWeb
https://twitter.com/TheNextWeb

The Wall Street Journal
@WSJ
https://twitter.com/WSJ

Tony Hsieh
@zappos
https://twitter.com/zappos

Topsy
@topsy
https://twitter.com/topsy

Tracky
@tracky
https://twitter.com/tracky

Triberr
@triberr
https://twitter.com/Triberr

Tweetdeck
@tweetdeck
https://twitter.com/TweetDeck

Twitter
@Twitter
https://twitter.com/twitter

USAToday
@USATODAY
https://twitter.com/USATODAY

Vine
@vineapp
https://twitter.com/vineapp

Visual.ly
@visually
https://twitter.com/Visually

Walmart
@walmart
https://twitter.com/walmart

Webstagram
@webstagram
https://twitter.com/webstagram

Whole Foods
@Wholefoods
https://twitter.com/WholeFoods

Wildfire
@wildfireapp
https://twitter.com/wildfireapp

WooBox
@woobox
https://twitter.com/woobox

YouTube
@youtube
https://twitter.com/YouTube

Zappos
@zappos
https://twitter.com/zappos